Cambridge Elements

Elements in the Philosophy of Mathematics
edited by
Penelope Rush
University of Tasmania
Stewart Shapiro
The Ohio State University

PHILOSOPHY OF MATHEMATICS FROM THE PYTHAGOREANS TO EUCLID

Barbara M. Sattler
Ruhr University Bochum

CAMBRIDGE
UNIVERSITY PRESS

Shaftesbury Road, Cambridge CB2 8EA, United Kingdom

One Liberty Plaza, 20th Floor, New York, NY 10006, USA

477 Williamstown Road, Port Melbourne, VIC 3207, Australia

314–321, 3rd Floor, Plot 3, Splendor Forum, Jasola District Centre,
New Delhi – 110025, India

103 Penang Road, #05-06/07, Visioncrest Commercial, Singapore 238467

Cambridge University Press is part of Cambridge University Press & Assessment, a department of the University of Cambridge.

We share the University's mission to contribute to society through the pursuit of education, learning and research at the highest international levels of excellence.

www.cambridge.org
Information on this title: www.cambridge.org/9781009578905

DOI: 10.1017/9781009122788

© Barbara M. Sattler 2025

This publication is in copyright. Subject to statutory exception and to the provisions of relevant collective licensing agreements, no reproduction of any part may take place without the written permission of Cambridge University Press & Assessment.

When citing this work, please include a reference to the DOI 10.1017/9781009122788

First published 2025

A catalogue record for this publication is available from the British Library

ISBN 978-1-009-57890-5 Hardback
ISBN 978-1-009-11406-6 Paperback
ISSN 2399-2883 (online)
ISSN 2514-3808 (print)

Cambridge University Press & Assessment has no responsibility for the persistence or accuracy of URLs for external or third-party internet websites referred to in this publication and does not guarantee that any content on such websites is, or will remain, accurate or appropriate.

For EU product safety concerns, contact us at Calle de José Abascal, 56, 1°, 28003 Madrid, Spain, or email eugpsr@cambridge.org

Philosophy of Mathematics from the Pythagoreans to Euclid

Elements in the Philosophy of Mathematics

DOI: 10.1017/9781009122788
First published online: April 2025

Barbara M. Sattler
Ruhr University Bochum

Author for correspondence: Barbara M. Sattler, barbara.sattler@rub.de

Abstract: This Element looks at the very beginning of the philosophy of mathematics in Western thought. It covers the first reflections on attempts to untie mathematics from its practical usage in administration, commerce, and land-surveying and discusses the first ideas to see mathematical structures as constituents underlying the physical world in the Pythagoreans. The first two sections focus on the epistemic status of mathematical knowledge in relation to philosophical knowledge and on the various ontological positions ancient Greek philosophers in early and classical times ascribe to mathematical objects – from independent and separate entities to mere abstractions and idealisations. Section 3 discusses the paradigmatic role mathematical deductions have played for philosophy, the role of mathematical diagrams, and mathematical methods of interest for philosophers. Section 4, finally, investigates a couple of individual concepts that are fundamental for both philosophy and mathematics, such as infinity.

Keywords: deductions, principles, numbers and geometrical objects, Plato, Aristotle, Euclid

© Barbara M. Sattler 2025

ISBNs: 9781009578905 (HB), 9781009114066 (PB), 9781009122788 (OC)
ISSNs: 2399-2883 (online), 2514-3808 (print)

Contents

Introduction   1

1 Ontology: What Kind of Things Are Mathematical Objects?   11

2 Epistemology: Mathematical Knowledge versus Philosophical Knowledge   25

3 Methodology   38

4 Central Concepts of Philosophy and Mathematics   52

References   69

Introduction

In contrast to Babylonian and Egyptian mathematics,[1] the older forerunners in the Mediterranean area, the focus of ancient Greek mathematics was not on applied but on theoretical mathematics. The Greeks were the first interested not only in the verification of results, but also in deductive proofs and justifications of the methods employed. Proof theory as a study of the structure of deductive proofs became a field of interest in its own right.[2] These features of ancient Greek mathematics already lend themselves to philosophical investigations and bring mathematics close to the general theoretical investigations that philosophy likewise is engaged with.

The difference in approach between Babylonian and Egyptian mathematics, on the one hand, and Greek mathematics on the other can already be seen if we compare mathematical problems students are given in textbooks.[3] First, the Babylonian and Egyptian traditions embed a mathematical task in a practical context; for example, they may ask their students to 'find the area of a silo', while an equivalent Greek text would ask the students to 'find the area of a cylinder' and thus show a much higher degree of abstraction. Furthermore, the Babylonian and Egyptian texts usually deal with an individual example using concrete numbers, the calculation of which is then shown.[4] For example, given a square field of 100 square cubits, a text asks the students to find the diameter of a round field of the same size, and then walks through the calculation and may verify the answer by calculating the area from the diameter. The student will then use the same procedure for similar problems. By contrast, Greek mathematics will state the objects abstractly with letter labels;[5] and instead of a verification of a particular result, there is a demonstration that everything so constructed will have the required property, which becomes the centrally important justification.

This focus on a theoretical investigation can also be seen in what were taken to be the three most important problems in Greek geometry and the way the Greeks dealt with them: (I) doubling the cube,[6] (II) trisecting an angle, and (III) squaring the circle.[7]

---

[1] For an overview, see Neugebauer (1969).
[2] The uniqueness of proof in Greek culture is, however, debated by historians of mathematics; see, for example, Chemla (2024) who also questions the dichotomy of proof and computation and gives interesting examples from ancient Chinese mathematics. We find what we may call proofs in Babylonian mathematics, but these are procedures and thus not demonstrative, and they do not seem to have been the mathematicians' focus.
[3] I owe the following example and important points of section I4 of this introduction to Henry Mendell.
[4] See Neugebauer (1969).   [5] See Netz (1999).
[6] Geometrically, this is a generalisation of the problem of doubling the square, which we will see in Section 2.
[7] We will see the last point with Euclid's method of exhaustion in Section 4. The first two problems were solved in algebra in the nineteenth century, while the third is transcendent and cannot be grasped by an algebraic equation.

In this introduction we will briefly look at the development of Greek mathematics out of a practical context and the demarcation of mathematics from other sciences. We will also touch upon one central theme within Greek mathematics: the relationship between geometry and arithmetic. That this is not simply an antiquated question can be seen from the fact that we today base our geometry on an arithmetical foundation. Finally, we will look at what to a modern mind may seem to be the main peculiarities of ancient Greek mathematics in general and the understanding of numbers in particular.

After this introduction[8], we will start in Section 1 of the body of the Element with a look at the kind of entities Greek philosophers took mathematical objects to be. Section 2 will show the role mathematical knowledge played for Greek philosophers. Section 3 will look at the paradigmatic role mathematical deductions have played for philosophy, the role of mathematical diagrams, and mathematical methods of interest for philosophers. Section 4, finally, investigates a couple of individual concepts that are fundamental for both philosophy and mathematics, such as infinity.

Timewise, we will cover the period from the beginning of ancient Greek mathematics and philosophising about it up to Plato, Aristotle, and Euclid: Plato and Aristotle are the first high point of philosophical thinking about mathematics, while Euclid marks the first high point in Greek mathematics. Euclid's *Elements* provide us with a large-scale systematisation of mathematical truth that builds on an axiomatic structure. But Euclid's *Elements* are not the first. This genre of literature, which attempts to present the current mathematical knowledge in a 'systematic' form for learners, seems to have been developed first by Hippocrates of Chios in the fifth century BCE. Euclid's *Elements* was, however, the most influential of these texts, presumably because of its large-scale architecture and its integration of the most important material from earlier mathematicians, such as Eudoxus and Theaetetus. As a consequence of the impact and range of Euclid's *Elements*, most of the earlier mathematical texts seem not to have been handed down any longer. This means very little is left of the earlier Greek mathematical texts, and so there are crucial blank spaces if we try to reconstruct the history of Greek mathematics. The oldest surviving Greek mathematical text is a long fragment of the quadratures of lunes by Hippocrates of Chios. It was contained in the *History of Geometry* written by Eudemus, a student of Aristotle, a work that itself is lost for the most part.[9]

As for the very beginning, there was perhaps some inkling of mathematics as a theoretical science in or around the time of Thales, if the ascription of that theorem to him has any basis. But Thales did not write anything, so there are no

---

[8] The sub-sections of the introductions are labelled I1-I5, while the main sections of the body of the Element are labeled 1-4.
[9] See von Fritz (1955), pp. 15–17 and Heath (1921), pp. 170–223.

Philosophy of Mathematics from the Pythagoreans to Euclid 3

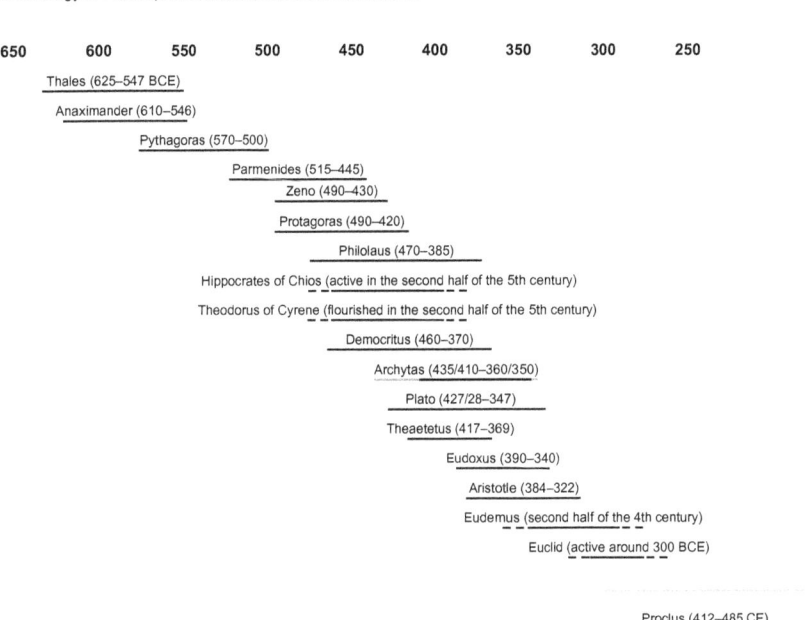

Figure 1 Chronology of Philosophers and Mathematicians mentioned. (Most of the dates are subject to some uncertainty.)

genuine fragments. Thus we will start with the Pythagoreans, where we definitively find some mathematical developments and have some fragments of the (later) Pythagoreans Philolaus and Archytas.

There are important mathematical developments happening after Euclid, for example, with Archimedes (285–212 BCE) and Apollonius of Perga (around 240–190 BCE); but we will not be able to look into these. As for later philosophers, the only one we will consult for a better understanding of the history of mathematics is Proclus (412–485 CE), who wrote an influential commentary on Euclid's *Elements* and seems to have drawn extensively on Eudemus' work (see Figure 1).

I1 The Development of Greek Mathematics: Detachment from a Practical Context

In spite of its theoretical focus, Greek mathematics had its origin in a practical context. Geometry derived from land-surveying and city-planning, as we can see already from the etymology of the English word 'geometry', which comes from the Greek word *geometria* and literally means 'measuring the earth' or 'land-surveying'. Herodotus claims in his *Histories* II, 109 that it is from the equal division of the land in Egypt that the Greeks learned *geometria*. And arithmetic was originally closely tied to administration and commerce – a connection against which Plato still argues as not covering the most important aspect of mathematics in *Republic* 525c–d.[10]

But very early on, Greek mathematics focused on mathematical characteristics as such, independent of any practical context. We will see in Section 3 in the body of this Element that it is only due to such a theoretical understanding of mathematics that irrationals were discovered – for practical purposes, the approximations we derive from measurements would have sufficed.

It seems that it was the abstraction of mathematical structure from the human practical context that made these structures also applicable to the understanding of nature and thus influenced the conceptualisation of the world – extending arithmetic and geometry to the universe as a whole. Thus, we also find the idea that mathematical structures are essential for the physical world early on. We will see in Section 1 later in this Element that, for the Pythagoreans, numbers and proportions constitute the universe, while for Plato geometrical forms as well as proportions are employed in the setup of the universe. And for Plato and many subsequent thinkers, the universe has to be spherical, because of the geometrical perfection of the sphere (which includes that all points on the surface have the same distance to the centre and that all the other Platonic solids can be inscribed in the sphere, in the way we see it in Kepler); the motions of the heavenly bodies accordingly have to be circular, which guarantees their intelligibility.

I2 Specific Demarcation of Mathematics in Ancient Greece

What did the Greeks in fact understand by mathematics? If we look at the Greek word from which our term 'mathematics' derives, *mathemata*, we see that it originally had a much broader meaning, indicating everything that is learnt, pieces or fields of knowledge. It encompasses all those subjects where we need to go through a certain course of steps in order to learn them and that hence may not be known by everyone.

It is in effect three generations of philosophers whose usage of the word eventually led to the meaning we are familiar with today: the Pythagoreans, Plato, and Aristotle. First, the Pythagoreans distinguish among their students between the *akousmatikoi* (the exoteric learners, who are only aware of the practical rules of conduct) and the *mathematikoi* (the esoteric learners who have

---

[10] For the practical and social origins of mathematics and questions such as how large a role the Greek culture of public debate and argumentation played in the development of mathematics, see Cuomo (2001), especially chapters 1 and 2.

gone through the full theory, or the advanced learners). And they also seem to have been the first to use 'mathematics' as a common name for arithmetic and geometry together. Secondly, Plato, in his depiction of the education of the future leaders of the ideal state in *Republic* VII, gives a curriculum that builds mainly on arithmetic, geometry, astronomy, and music for the advanced learners; which are thus the *mathemata* to be learned. Finally, Aristotle divides the theoretical sciences – the first division we find in Western thought – into first philosophy (metaphysics/theology), physics (natural philosophy), and mathematics (see, e.g., *Metaphysics* 1026a18–19).

This long process of coining the meaning of the word also reflects the fact that mathematics and philosophy are usually understood to derive from the same origin, which was in general seen as wisdom.[11] It is not clear when mathematics separated off from this, but it was one of the first, if not *the* first, science to do so. Accordingly, it seems to be its own field already in the fifth century BCE, and could be seen as paradigmatic for other sciences, as we will see later in Section 2 in the main body of the Element. As such, mathematics seems to have influenced philosophy by the rigour of its argumentation, by building a system starting from a couple of basic axioms, and by its use of deductions. And it also became an important subject of philosophical reflections for the question of what is essential for a science.

Among the sixth-century Presocratics, we find several philosopher-mathematicians, like the Pythagoreans and perhaps also Thales. Likewise, in the fifth and fourth centuries BCE we find thinkers working in both fields, such as the atomist Democritus, who wrote on conic sections, and the Pythagoreans Philolaus and Archytas. And Plato's Academy seems to have been a centre where not only were philosophers trained, but also mathematical research was performed by people like Eudoxus and Theaetetus. A sign reading 'Let no one ignorant of geometry enter here' was allegedly placed over the entrance to the Academy. Plato himself saw mathematics at times as paradigmatic, at others as propaedeutic for philosophy. Aristotle also took mathematics as paradigmatic for philosophy in its method in certain respects, but distinguished it from first philosophy and physics by its objects – mathematical objects are changeless, but have no existence independent of empirical things. The Hellenistic philosopher Epicurus, however, excluded mathematics from the sciences as having no practical relevance, and for the Stoics likewise it was not central.

Which mathematical sciences belong to mathematics in ancient Greece? For the most part the four disciplines arithmetic, geometry, astronomy, and music are seen

---

[11] Salmon (1980) talks about the 'twin origin of philosophy and geometry'; see also Heath (1921), p. 3.

as constituting the mathematical sciences, a quartet we find first in the Pythagorean Archytas and in Plato's *Republic*.[12] In the Middle Ages they became the quadrivium, which together with the trivium formed the basis for liberal education at universities. Aristotle, however, groups astronomy and harmonics, together with optics, as the more 'physical' branches of mathematics.[13] These latter sciences especially are close to natural philosophy for Aristotle.

An understanding of ancient mathematics faces the additional problem that the ancient Greeks distinguished between arithmetic and what they call *logistikê* – a distinction not known to modern mathematics. There are different interpretations of this distinction, but for the most part, arithmetic is understood as dealing with number theory and *logistikê* as the art of calculation.[14]

Finally, it is an interesting question whether the ancient Greeks thought that there exists a general mathematical science or not – here it seems philosophers and mathematicians come apart. The first text where we find the idea of a general mathematics discussed comes from Aristotle, who claims that universal mathematics applies to all mathematical kinds (*Metaphysics* 1026a27); scholars have usually understood him to be referring to Eudoxus' theory of proportion which holds for different mathematical sciences. What is left open is the question whether general mathematics possesses its own specific subject (perhaps something like pure quantity) or not.[15] But we do not seem to find any such universal mathematics in Euclid. Euclid's concern for homogeneity indicates that he thinks of a proposition in Book V as a unified formulation for a number of analogous propositions concerning particular magnitudes like lines, planes, and so on. He does not seem to think of it as a single proposition about more abstract objects like magnitudes or quantities as such, and he treats proportions in geometry and in the arithmetical books separately. Euclid is, however, also not interested in discussing the metaphysical basis for the applicability of propositions, but only in reasons to believe them.

I3 Relationship between Geometry and Arithmetic

Although geometry, arithmetic, music, and astronomy were seen as the main mathematical sciences, we will concentrate on geometry and arithmetic in this Element, which is also what Euclid's *Elements* focuses on. While we can clearly understand, for example, Books I–IV of Euclid's *Elements* as plane geometry, and Books VII–IX as concerning arithmetic, it is less clear how exactly

---

[12] Where solid geometry is added as a fifth.
[13] *Physics* 194a8; for the classification of mathematics, see also Heath (1921), pp. 10ff.
[14] See Heath (1921), pp. 13–16.
[15] For details, see Mendell (2004). See also Aristotle, *Metaphysics* M, 3; K, 7; and *Posterior Analytics* I, 5.

geometry and arithmetic were defined and in which relation they were seen to each other. We may think of modern geometry as a study of spatial structures, but ancient Greek mathematics seems to treat it as a study of magnitudes, more precisely of figures. And while we seem to get a neat division of Greek mathematics into the study of multitude or discrete quantity, namely arithmetic, and the study of magnitude or continuous quantity, namely geometry, it is unclear whether it was conceptualised like this before Aristotle's *Categories*.[16]

In spite of hints of a universal mathematics, Aristotle usually treats geometry and arithmetic as two different sciences that differ in their genus. Their exact relationship was a matter of intensive dispute, which is connected with the question of a possible superiority of one over the other. (This also concerns questions like whether the operations of addition, subtraction, multiplication, division, and so on are geometrical or arithmetical.)

In contrast to Babylonian and Egyptian mathematics, Greek mathematics sometime in the fifth century BCE started to geometrise mathematics, performing mathematical proofs from then onwards mainly in geometrical terms (presumably since certain topics, like incommensurability, could only be dealt with geometrically, and arithmetic could not handle fractions).[17] Thus at least since 400 BCE geometry was dominant vis-à-vis arithmetic in Western mathematics, a dominance that lasted until early modern times. It is also reflected in the fact that Euclid's *Elements* shows a much more systematically developed geometry than arithmetic, giving many results and procedures in geometrical terms that we would give in arithmetical ones. Furthermore, Euclid represents numbers by lines, and what we understand as arithmetic operations, such as addition and subtraction, he seems to understand in geometrical terms (e.g., what we would think of as adding number x to number y Euclid represents as extending a line AB by the length of line CD).[18] Geometrical terminology is used for arithmetic, for example, when in Book VII, definitions 16 and 17, the result of two numbers having been multiplied is called a plane number, and that of three numbers having been multiplied a solid number.

In philosophical reflection, however, we find different assessments of the relationship between arithmetic and geometry. For the most part, arithmetic is seen as superior. The Pythagorean Archytas calls it superior to geometry and other sciences in DK47B4, because it treats its objects in a clearer way and 'brings

---

[16] That we cannot simply presuppose such a distinction from the very beginning is clear also from the fact that the Pythagoreans represented numbers with the help of pebbles and, keeping the extension of the pebbles in mind, seem to have treated numbers in part like magnitudes. See Sattler (2020a), p. 293.
[17] The arithmetic-geometric problem of doubling the square has a possible geometric solution for the Greeks (i.e., the diagonal) but no arithmetic one.
[18] See, e.g., *Elements* IX, 21–27; and also Mueller (1969), pp. 302–304. But see Unguru (1975) for a different understanding. There are only a few traces of calculation procedures in Euclid's arithmetic.

proofs to completion where geometry leaves them out'.[19] And for Aristotle arithmetic is prior, more exact, and simpler than geometry, since it is based on fewer things.[20] His example in *Posterior Analytics* is a point in geometry, which, like a unit in arithmetic, is a basic being, but in addition also has a position, so that it involves more features than the arithmetical unit. The greater simplicity and accuracy of arithmetic brings it closer to first principles than geometry for Aristotle and thus demonstrates the superiority of arithmetic over geometry.

The Pythagorean Philolaus, however, calls geometry the source and mother-city of the other mathematical sciences in DK44A7a and thus seems to assume geometry to be superior to arithmetic. This raises the question whether the differences in assessment of their relationship derives from a different point of view or from a development within mathematics. The latter suggestion has sometimes been connected with the fact that within ancient Greek mathematics, arithmetic seems to have been more prominent in the beginning before the geometrisation of mathematics in the fifth century (for example, Szabó (2004) understands Archytas' claim of the superiority of *logistikê* as depicting an older Pythagorean attitude dominant before the geometrical turn). Against this developmental thesis, however, speaks the fact that Aristotle, quite some time after any geometrical turn, claims arithmetic to be superior. And also the Pythagoreans were not unified in this respect, since Archytas, living in the first half of the fourth century, claims arithmetic to be superior, while Philolaus, a generation older than him, claims this for geometry. So it is more likely that these different assessments are due to different points of view – the mathematicians tending to geometry since this is the more powerful discipline within ancient Greek mathematics, and philosophers tending to arithmetic since its basis seems to be closer to first scientific principles.[21] In any case, the tension between the status of arithmetic and geometry led to general ontological and epistemological questions, some of which we will see in the first two main sections.

I4 Specificities of Greek Mathematics

While much more abstract than Babylonian mathematics, ancient Greek mathematics is much less abstract than modern mathematics, and the abstraction we find in ancient mathematics is of a very different sort than our modern one.

---

[19] See also Huffmann (2005), pp. 225–252. The greater clarity of arithmetic may become obvious if we look, for example, at proposition IV, 10 in Euclid's *Elements*: 'To construct an isosceles triangle having each of the angles at the base double of the remaining one'. Arithmetically this is relatively simple to solve: $2x + x/2 = 180$; thus $x = 72$; while Euclid gives a rather complicated drawing. Given that Archytas talks in fact about *logistikê* in this fragment, not about arithmetic, he may, however, only be thinking about it working technically more quickly.

[20] *Posterior Analytics*, I, 27, 87a34–37; *Metaphysics*, A, 2, 982a26–28 and M, 3, 1078a9ff.

[21] See Mueller (1969). It is unclear why we find the difference in assessment in the Pythagoreans.

Thus, when we talk about the philosophy of ancient Greek mathematics, we should be aware that with *mathematics* we are talking about a somewhat different beast than when we refer to modern mathematics.[22]

Greek mathematics has a certain level of abstraction in that it is interested in general mathematical features as such; it is, for the most part, non-metrical, that is, it does not use numbers for general mathematical problems, and it is independent of any concrete practical context. But ancient Greek geometry is much closer to perception in its reliance on diagrammatic representations than its modern pendant. It is pre-algebraic, pre-structural, and pre-set theoretic.[23]

Ancient Greek mathematics does not employ functional variables, but only parameters (and proportions) – so while for certain operations we can freely chose a value, once it is chosen it always has to be the same value and cannot vary. Infinity is in part presupposed by ancient Greek mathematicians, without, however, taking up the fundamental discussions about this concept we find in the philosophers. And, as we can see in Euclid, Greek mathematics of classical and early Hellenistic times gives us only the minimal meta-language to connect arguments – it is only philosophers who deal with meta-reflections. Let us finally have a closer look at the Greek understanding of numbers.

I5 Notion of Numbers

Number theory started in what we may consider as a systematic way in ancient Greek mathematics. Books VII–IX of Euclid's *Elements* provide us with a definition of primes, an algorithm for computing the greatest common divisor of two numbers (what we now call the Euclidean algorithm; VII, 2), and the first known proof of the infinitude of primes (IX, 20).

But there are three important differences in the ancient Greek understanding of numbers to modern accounts:

(1) First, a number is a collection of units; it is defined as 'multitude composed of units' (*Elements* VII, 2). The number seven, for example, is a collection of seven units.[24]
(2) Second, 1 is for the most part not seen as a number, but as the beginning or principle (*archê*) of number, what defines the unit. 1 is not a number in the

---

[22] For ancient philosophers, it is seen as focusing on the same world as other theoretical sciences are – for example, for Aristotle both mathematics and physics deal with the empirical world, just with different aspects, and for Plato both mathematics and other theoretical sciences deal with intelligible structures.
[23] The idea of structure, essential in modern mathematics, plays no role in ancient mathematics; see Mueller (1969), p. 299.
[24] Accordingly, Euclid starts his definitions in the arithmetical books with defining a unit, and only afterwards a number (VII, definitions 1 and 2).

way 3 and 4 are, since the 1 determines what we count (1 defines the unit with which we count, for example, *book*, and then we count how many books there are in my room).[25] So there is a strong difference between 1 and numbers. We see that units thus serve double-duty – they are the constituents of each number and they determine the one that is the basis for counting.

(3) Finally, for the Greeks, numbers mean positive integers, so we are dealing with a theory of natural numbers; other numbers are not known. Irrational numbers, like $\sqrt{2}$, are not numbers for the Greeks, but proportions between magnitudes, since they can deal with them only geometrically, not arithmetically. Number in itself implies rationality and countability for the Greeks.

While Babylonian and Egyptian mathematics used fractions, there were no real fractions in Greek mathematics up to Archimedes in the third century BCE (apart from ⅔ in a practical context). Greek mathematicians took the 1 as indivisible unity, so that there could not be any fractions;[26] instead, they used proportions and submultiples. Submultiples allow us to treat fractions as multiples of a more basic unit; for example, if I have $1/7$, I can understand one as a basic unit which I have to take seven times to get to the old basic unit. The expression "$1/7$" thus gives me two different units and indicates a mathematical operation (the relation of the smaller to the bigger unit), not a number.

Numbers are not defined in terms of successor functions or by what they allow us to do and they are not sets. Instead they are understood as a quantified plurality of things of some sort. Numbers used in ordinary life are seen as tied to a concrete group of things (for example, a three of cups, if I am counting my cups). And what is sometimes called 'mathematical number', that is, the numbers mathematicians deal with, is tied to a *monas*, namely a mathematical unit (which is what Euclid refers to in his definition of numbers).[27]

The ancient Greeks also investigated which further features characterise numbers. This can be seen especially in the discussion about oddness and evenness of numbers and of prime numbers. The Greeks not only distinguished between odd and even numbers, but also even-times odd numbers,[28] even-times even numbers, and so on. And they not only discuss prime numbers, but also numbers prime *to each other*.[29] The number 2 is an especially interesting case,

---

[25] See Klein (1968), chapter 6.
[26] See Plato *Republic* 525d–e; Aristotle's *Metaphysics* Iota claims that the one is *treated* as indivisible; see Sattler (2020a), chapter 8.
[27] For the Pythagoreans, mathematical numbers are made up not of abstract units, but of units having magnitudes.
[28] That is, a number of the form $2(2m + 1)$; see Euclid VII, def. 9.
[29] I.e. numbers 'measured by a unit alone as a common measure'. We think of prime numbers as the most basic building blocks of our number system and thus of their effects, while the ancients think more about how numbers themselves can be characterised.

for it is an even number for Plato and Aristotle, and a prime number for Aristotle and Euclid.[30] It is, however, neither even nor prime for the Pythagoreans, but constitutes, together with the 1, the first principles of all numbers; and for other mathematicians, like Nicomachus, being a prime number is a sub-division of odd numbers.

Early Greek mathematics represented numbers by pebbles,[31] while later on numbers were represented by lines, which is also what we find in Euclid's arithmetical books. Like the Egyptians, the Greeks used a decimal system (in contrast to the Babylonians, who used also a sexagesimal system). And the Greeks used two numerical systems with different advantages and disadvantages: the Herodiadic and the ordinary Ionic alphabetical numerals.[32]

1 Ontology: What Kind of Things Are Mathematical Objects?

This section will investigate what kind of entities Greek philosophers took mathematical objects to be. We will see that their debates prefigure some of the most important ontological positions in current debates, such as Platonism,[33] abstractionism, and, according to some scholars, also fictionalism. Following roughly Aristotle's analysis in *Metaphysics* M,[34] we can say that the main distinction in determining the ontological status of mathematical objects is whether or not they are seen as having their own existence, independent of either the world or human minds. If they have an independent existence, they could either exist *separately* – here we are heading towards Platonism – or exist nevertheless in physical things – this is a position we will find with the Pythagoreans. By contrast, Aristotle understands mathematical entities as dependent on physical things; he holds a version of abstractionism.

This section will start with the Pythagorean assumption that numbers exist in perceptible objects; but rather than being dependent on these objects, numbers constitute them. We will then move on to the position of Plato, who also understands mathematical objects as independent of the physical world, but as existing separately. More exactly speaking we will discuss two central ontological claims concerning mathematical objects in Plato: first the claim of the *Phaedo* and the *Republic* that mathematical objects, like numbers or equality,

---

[30] *Topics* 157b and *Elements* VII, definition 12.
[31] See Simplicius (2002), *In Phys.* 457 and KRS (1983), p. 337 for a depiction.
[32] For details, see Heath (1921), pp. 26–64.
[33] Even if Plato himself understood mathematical objects, as we will see, somewhat differently from how they are understood in modern Platonism as we find it, for instance, in Gödel or, arguably, in Frege.
[34] Aristotle's *Metaphysics* deals with the most fundamental beings, things, and principles there are; Books M and N discuss whether there are unmoved eternal Beings and if so, whether mathematical entities belong to this group.

are entities that exist separately as part of an intelligible realm. Secondly, the idea in the *Timaeus* that geometrical bodies, which are themselves made up of perfect triangles, underlie the four physical elements earth, water, air, and fire, and are thus the building blocks of physical things. The position of the *Timaeus* may sound somewhat Pythagorean, except that it is not numbers but geometrical figures that constitute the physical things and thus also exist in them.[35] However, in the Platonic picture the geometrical forms come into play once *Timaeus*'s creator god applies them to the chaotic material world – accordingly, these geometrical figures exist before, and originally also separate from, the physical world.

A stark contrast to the Platonic and Pythagorean metaphysics of mathematics will finally be found in Aristotle's understanding of mathematical objects as abstractions and, perhaps, idealisations of the physical ones. For Aristotle, mathematical objects are thus dependent on the physical world from which they are derived and which grounds them ontologically. With Euclid, finally, we do not get any explicit ontological commitment. But we may wonder what ontological implications claims like '*let there be* a square ABCD' ('*Estô tetragônon to ABCD*') have.[36]

1.1 Numbers as the Ultimate Constituents of Things with the Pythagoreans

When we look at early Pythagoreanism, we will distinguish between those Pythagoreans that Aristotle discusses in his *Metaphysics* and the earliest Pythagoreans of whom we possess reliable fragments, namely Philolaus, a contemporary of Socrates, and Archytas, a contemporary of Plato.[37] We will start with the Pythagoreans as reported by Aristotle and then continue on to Philolaus.[38]

---

[35] Accordingly, the main interlocutor of this dialogue, Timaeus, has often been seen as a Pythagorean.

[36] Is it purely meant as something we should imagine in our head? Does it assume that there are squares in the world around us? Or may those scholars be right who have toyed with the idea that Euclid was related to the Platonic Academy and thus assumed 'squares existing in themselves'? The first three postulates of Book I have sometimes been read as postulating the existence of straight lines and circles (see Heath (1921), p. 374 and Acerbi (2013), p. 681), but they do not tell us what kind of existence they have. Mueller (1981), by contrast, understands the magnitudes dealt with in the *Elements* as abstractions from objects that leave out all properties apart from quantity, and mathematical units as leaving out all properties of objects apart from self-identity and numerosity.

[37] It is unclear how exactly the fragments we have from the group Aristotle calls 'the Pythagoreans' relate to Archytas and Philolaus: they may reflect Aristotle's interpretation of Philolaus or Aristotle may indeed distinguish between the older Pythagoreanism and the Platonised Pythagoreanism prevalent at his time; so there may have been genuinely different positions among the Pythagoreans.

[38] Philolaus did not use numbers, but limiters and unlimiteds as principles.

Philosophy of Mathematics from the Pythagoreans to Euclid 13

Aristotle reports in his *Metaphysics* that the Pythagoreans assume mathematical objects to exist *in* perceptible objects and that their principles and elements are the principles and elements of the sensible world:

> [T]he Pythagoreans, as they are called, devoted themselves to mathematics; they were the first to advance this study, and having been brought up in it, they thought its principles were the principles of all things. Since of these principles numbers are by nature the first, and in numbers they seemed to see many resemblances to the things that exist and come into being [...] since, again, they saw that the attributes and the ratios of the musical scales were expressible in numbers; since, then, all other things seemed in their whole nature to be modelled after numbers, and numbers seemed to be the first things in the whole of nature, they supposed the elements of numbers to be the elements of all things, and the whole heaven to be a musical scale and a number (985b23–986a3).

> But the Pythagoreans, because they saw many attributes of numbers belonging to sensible bodies, supposed real things to be numbers – not separable numbers, however, but numbers of which real things consist. But why? Because the attributes of numbers are present in a musical scale and in the heavens and in many other things (1090a20–25).

So for the Pythagoreans, mathematical properties (presumably properties like being quantifiable, being of odd or even number) can be found in sensible phenomena, in whatever we empirically observe. This seems to have led them to infer that sensible bodies either consist of numbers or are phenomena of numbers in some way. While Plato's idealism and Aristotle's abstractionism may strike us as not true but plausible or at least intelligible, some readers may simply be flabbergasted by this Pythagorean position. However, it seems to have been a very early (if very specialised) position in Greek mathematics and philosophy and features of this position have been taken up repeatedly in the history of thought, most recently perhaps by Baron (2021), who calls his suggestion that the important properties of mathematical entities are structural and as such also to be found in the physical world a 'Pythagorean proposal'. Let us look at possible reasons for the Pythagorean position.

It may be seen as answering the puzzle how it can be that numbers follow their own rules (independent of the physical world), but yet are applicable to the sensible realm to the degree that mathematical statements are true of the world.[39] This combination would be possible, according to a Pythagorean picture, if

---

[39] At least this is a puzzle to which we will see different answers in Plato's *Timaeus* and in Aristotle later and it seems plausible that the Pythagoreans may have raised this question. It is unclear whether the Pythagorean idea of numbers 'constituting' things is meant to suggest numbers to be physical elements or principles of things.

mathematical objects are in the world and *constitute* sensible bodies – as such constituents, numbers can be understood independently but are yet immediately connected with the perceptible world.

The applicability of mathematics to the physical world is shown with the example of music and astronomy. There seems to be one phenomenon in particular mentioned in our two quotations that led to the idea that numbers constitute things: musical scales and harmonies. It is, after all, not the relationship of this very string to that very string that constitutes an octave, but the relationship between every pair of strings whose lengths are in a relation of 1:2. So it ultimately seems to be the relationship of 1:2 (which can be realised in different materials that can vibrate so as to produce a sound) which constitutes the octave. But if numerical ratios underlie musical intervals, they may also underlie other perceptible things and phenomena which display mathematical features.

The preceding passages suggest a strong interpretation of the idea that numbers underlie the sensible world in the sense that numbers are indeed seen as the ultimate constituents and essence of sensible things.[40] Aristotle claims that for the Pythagoreans, numbers are not only the principles of everything but also that the whole of nature is 'modelled after numbers'.

But there is also a weaker interpretation available for the idea that mathematical structures underlie the physical world[41] – an interpretation that may be displayed by some fragments of the Pythagorean Philolaus, who claims that 'all things that are known have numbers. For it is not possible for anything to be thought of or known without this' (DK44B4).

Philolaus here is not making a claim about the whole universe, but about all things that can be known (which may or may not have the same extension as the whole universe). And these things are not said to *be* number, but only to *have* number (in contrast to the picture in Plato's *Timaeus*, they themselves possess numbers, rather than have numbers bestowed upon them). The basic idea seems to be that we can have knowledge of things, and our reason essentially works with numbers, so there has to be something numerical about the things known (for example, that they are quantifiable). Here numbers are a necessary condition for knowledge and because things we know have them, mathematical operations are presumably also applicable to these things. But it is left open how strong the ontological commitment is that is entailed in the idea of 'having a number' – it may simply mean that physical things have a quantitative aspect,

---

[40] See also fragment DK58A10. In *Metaphysics* 987b8f. Aristotle also claims that the Pythagoreans understand sensible things as imitations of numbers.

[41] The strong interpretation may seem similar to modern accounts that think everything *is* in fact a code; while a weaker interpretation may be shown when people talk as if a graph, or numerical depiction, is not simply a depiction, but the thing talked about.

Philosophy of Mathematics from the Pythagoreans to Euclid 15

or that they are a unity composed of a number of parts.[42] And while the fact that numbers are tied to the knowability of things suggests that they are not tied to some accidental feature, it is left open whether there may also be other features we can know about things, for example, some quality, that may be something over and above the fundamental knowledge we have based on numbers.

Three points seem to be in the background of the Pythagorean assumption that things either have numbers or are even constituted by numbers: first, the wide-spread understanding in ancient Greece that numbers are multiples of a certain unit, usually of concrete things,[43] and thus closely linked to the perceptible world; secondly, a peculiarity of the Pythagoreans, that numbers are seen as generated;[44] and finally, the Pythagorean idea that there is a cause for the separation and distinction of the number series – their discreteness is accounted for or grounded by the void.[45] Thinking of numbers as requiring void to separate them suggests understanding numbers along the lines of bodily stuff. And it fits the fact that the Pythagoreans conceived of numbers with the help of pebbles. Accordingly, when they claim that physical things are constituted out of numbers, this must also be seen against the background of a more physical understanding of numbers. Aristotle, however, thinks that the Pythagorean position confuses the indivisibility of numerical units with the indivisibility of physical things and accordingly faces two problems: first, it leads to the assumption of atoms (indivisibles) of a sort, and Aristotle attempts to show in his *Physics* that atomism gets us into problems if assumed for the physical world[46] and destroys mathematics (for then a mathematician could not cut a line wherever she needs to, but only where atoms allow); second, it remains unclear how numerical units, which in themselves have no physical magnitude and weight, can make up something with a physical magnitude and weight.[47]

---

[42] Or constituted out of Philolaus' most basic principles, the unlimiteds and limiters; see Huffmann (1993).

[43] So (with the exception of mathematical numbers) there is no talk of three as such, but three apples, three stars, etc.

[44] Aristotle strongly opposes this idea, which for him means not understanding the eternity of numbers (*Metaphysics* 1091a12–22).

[45] Aristotle, *Physics* 213b22–27, DK58B30. Numbers are not, as for us, simply a paradigm of discreteness.

[46] E.g., in *Physics* VI, 12 Aristotle shows that there cannot be atoms, since we can always divide things further at least conceptually – otherwise, at some point we could not account for differences in speed any longer.

[47] Aristotle, *Metaphysics* M, 8, 1083b8–19. Aristotle seems to entertain two different interpretations of the Pythagorean position: first, that they talk in fact about a heaven and bodies different from the perceptible ones (*Metaphysics* N, 3, 1090a20–35). Second, that they assume the units of numbers to possess spatial extension (*Metaphysics* M, 6, 1080b16ff.), which is in conflict with Aristotle's assumption that the numbers the mathematicians work with are abstract numbers and thus without any extension and weight.

Moving on to Plato's account of mathematics now, we will encounter two of his central ontological claims concerning mathematical objects: (a) the claim that mathematical objects are entities with their own independent existence, and (b) the idea in the *Timaeus* that geometrical bodies, which are themselves made up of perfect triangles, underlie the four elements and are thus the building blocks of physical things. The first claim (a) derives from a discussion about the question what ontological status mathematical objects have which Plato raises explicitly in his *Republic*, and to some degree also in his *Phaedo*. It seems to hold true of mathematical objects in general, but the emphasis seems to be on arithmetic. And so we learn of numbers not only that numbers as such exist independently of the physical world, but also that the many instances of each individual number which the mathematicians use for their calculations are intermediates between the sensible and the intelligible objects. The second claim (b) derives from the attempt in the *Timaeus* to explain the perceptible world as something that can be known, that is intelligible. The focus here is on geometry, but proportions are also understood to underlie the orbits of the motions of the heavenly bodies.

1.2 Mathematical Objects as Part of the Intelligible Realm in Plato's *Republic* and *Phaedo*

Aristotle, Plato's main opponent with respect to the ontology of mathematical objects, provides us with a rationale for the assumption of separately existing mathematical entities in his *Metaphysics* 1090a35–b1: those thinkers who make numbers exist separately, like Plato, do so because axioms do not seem to hold of perceptible things, but yet are true in themselves.

In his example of the line, that we will discuss in the next section, Plato assumes mathematical objects to exist separately as intelligible entities that are not derived from the perceptible world (even though mathematicians use sensible objects as examples). But his mathematical ontology is in fact more complex than that. For the main claim by Plato and many Platonists about mathematical entities, namely that they exist not only independently of physical entities but also separately in an intelligible realm, leaves it open how to think of this logical space. And this separate logical space is not necessarily the same as the logical space of Platonic Forms. We get a distinction among mathematical entities between those that behave very much like Forms, and those that are the tools of the mathematicians that have an intermediate status between Forms and sensible things. Let me explain this a bit more with respect to its most prominent example, the distinction between what is commonly called Form numbers and mathematical numbers.[48]

Forms are, roughly speaking, separately existing universals (Beauty as such) that are eternal, immutable, simple, and existing on their own.[49] In the same way in which on a Platonic account there is a Form of Justice, and a Form of Equality, there seems to be a Form of twoness (*Phaedo* 101c) – the Form of two is what it means to be two. Every pair, and every 2 I use, participates in twoness. Being a Form also implies that there can be only one of it.[50] No mathematical operation is defined on the Form number, since this would not fit with Forms existing independently. In addition to Form numbers, there are also the numbers the mathematicians work with when they multiply, for example, two times two. Of these there has to be a plurality and operations need to be defined on them, otherwise our arithmetical practises would not be possible. For the Platonists, we thus need to have one intelligible object that grounds twoness of which there can only be one, the Form number, and another one that can be an object of mathematical operations and of which there can be a plurality, mathematical numbers.[51]

These mathematical numbers are also independent of the sensible two I write in the sand and of concrete pairs in the perceptible world; if, let us say, we were living in a world which contained only five items, a mathematician could still calculate what is six times six, even if no items corresponded to this operation in the perceptible world. Accordingly, mathematical numbers seem to be treated as so-called intermediates:[52] they possess an ontological status in between the individual intelligible single Forms and the many perceptible things, since they are many, like the perceptible things, but yet intelligible and not sensible, like the Forms.[53] The full Platonic story in fact even seems to contain four kinds of

---

[48] Aristotle in his *Metaphysics* M gives us a division of the metaphysical positons in Plato's Academy according to which some, like Plato himself, took there to be Form numbers and mathematical numbers; others assumed only mathematical numbers – a position usually ascribed to Speusippus – and finally some, like Xenocrates, tried to identify both Form numbers and mathematical numbers.

[49] This holds true of the middle Plato, while the late Plato, in his *Sophist*, assumes Forms to be complex. The fact that Forms seem to self-predicate – for example, the Form of the Beautiful is not only the reason for all sensible things to be beautiful, but is also itself the perfect paradigm of what it is a Form of, of what it means to be beautiful – has led scholars to question whether Platonic Forms are indeed universals in our sense.

[50] Since a single Form is meant to be responsible for the same feature in different things.

[51] Similarly, there seems to be only one Form of a circle, but the mathematicians deal with several, for example, when comparing the relationship of the diameter of a circle to its area to that of another circle.

[52] See *Metaphysics* 1090b35–36.

[53] See also Proclus (1992), who opens his commentary on Euclid with the claim that the mathematical objects occupy a middle place between the indivisible Forms and the things that are through and through divisible. Mendell (2022), p. 359 claims these intermediates to be the ancestors of mathematical Platonism, since mathematical propositions are true of these objects.

'twos': (1) the perceptible pairs in the world, (2) the mathematical numbers which are used in mathematical operations, (3) the Form number two, and finally (4) the indefinite two (or dyad) which Aristotle reports to function as the principle of plurality in Plato's unwritten doctrine.[54]

1.3 Mathematical Objects as Underlying the Physical Realm in Plato's *Timaeus*

We saw that with the Pythagoreans, mathematical objects constitute the physical world. And also according to Plato's *Timaeus*, mathematical objects exist in the world – geometrical bodies underlie the physical phenomena we perceive. In contrast to the Pythagoreans, it is not numbers but geometrical bodies that Plato sees employed. Moreover, these mathematical objects used in the Platonic universe originally exist separately from the physical world and are thus independent of it; the geometrical solids are used to bestow order onto the originally given chaos and to transform it into a regular cosmos.

The *Timaeus* is Plato's cosmology and most encompassing account of the natural world –from the microstructure of the atomistic particles underlying the basic elements of the world all the way up to the arrangement of the heavenly bodies. It gives an account of how our cosmos was shaped by a divine demiurge out of an independently existing space-like receptacle which is filled with traces of the physical elements. Our physical universe is seen as understandable[55] because the demiurge builds it by imitating an intelligible model; and he does so by using mathematical structures in order to imbue the irregular traces of the chaotically moving elements with order and measure. It is in three areas that the demiurge uses mathematical structures: (a) proportions are used for connecting all the physical material there is in the world body, thus securing the unity of the world body, and for determining the order according to which the fabric of the world soul and thus also the orbits of the heavenly bodies are formed (*Timaeus* 31b–32c and 35b–36d); (b) the number series is employed for measuring the motions of sensible objects (39b–d); and finally (c) the material atoms are built from geometrical bodies (53a–55e);[56] we will concentrate on this last point.

Before the divine demiurge starts his work, there are only traces of the four so-called elements (53b). With these four elements, fire, air, water, and earth, Plato takes up what in the physical investigations of his time was seen as the material

---

[54] See *Physics* 203a4–16. In *Metaphysics* N, 3 Aristotle ascribes a threefold ontology to Plato: perceptible numbers, mathematical numbers, and Form numbers (1090b32–36), while in Plato's dialogues we find only hints of such a three- or fourfold ontology. In contrast to modern 'Platonism', this ontology does not contain the set of all pairs.

[55] At least to the degree that a probable account (an *eikos mythos*) is possible.

[56] For a more detailed account, see Sattler (2012) and (2020a), chapter 6.

foundation of the perceptible world, while he also wants to make clear that these are not really the most basic elements there are. For they themselves are made up of geometrical bodies. Originally there are solely unintelligible traces of the elements. It is only with the work of the demiurge that order and measure are introduced into the world, so that the presumably crooked surfaces of these elemental traces are formed into straight ones that make up the surfaces of geometrical bodies.[57] The geometrical bodies the demiurge chooses as the basis for the physical 'elements' are the most regular (and thus most 'beautiful') solids, what we have come to call 'Platonic bodies'[58] – tetrahedron, cube, octahedron, icosahedron, and dodecahedron. Here Plato seems to have employed new mathematical research of his time, presumably undertaken by Theaetetus, that showed that there can only be five convex polyhedra that are fully regular in the sense that all faces are congruent regular polygons and the same number of faces meet at every vertex.[59] This research showed the exhaustiveness of these regular polyhedra which Plato took up as a suitable basis for material 'elements'.

Thinking of bodies in a mathematical way, Timaeus claims that these geometrical solids are composed of basic surfaces – of triangles. As there is no single kind of triangle out of which all the Platonic solids can be constructed, it is assumed that the demiurge uses two different kinds of triangles: the isosceles right-angled triangle out of which the surfaces of the cube are formed, and the half-equilateral triangle as a basis for the tetrahedron, the octahedron, and the icosahedron (see Figure 2). So the real 'elements' (in the sense of the basic foundation of everything there is in the sensible world) are not fire, air, water, and earth, but two kinds of triangles; and Plato leaves it explicitly open whether there may be some even simpler elements out of which these surfaces of the world are originally formed, such as lines.

The different geometrical solids are ascribed to the four elements according to the following kind of similarity: as the cube has the most stable base (given its surface area), it is the basis of earth, which is the most immobile of the elements; whereas the body with the fewest faces must be the most mobile and the lightest, thus the tetrahedron underlies fire.

While a single geometrical solid underlying the physical elements is too small to be seen, an aggregated mass of them is perceptible. And, as in the case of other atomistic accounts, what we then perceive is not simply an aggregate of atoms, for example, not a bunch of mathematical tetrahedra, but the phenomenon we are used to, fire. In contrast to merely mathematical tetrahedra, the tetrahedra

---

[57] See Sattler (2012), p. 180.
[58] They are so called because Plato's *Timaeus* is the first text to mention them.
[59] See the proof in Euclid's *Elements* XIII, proposition 18.

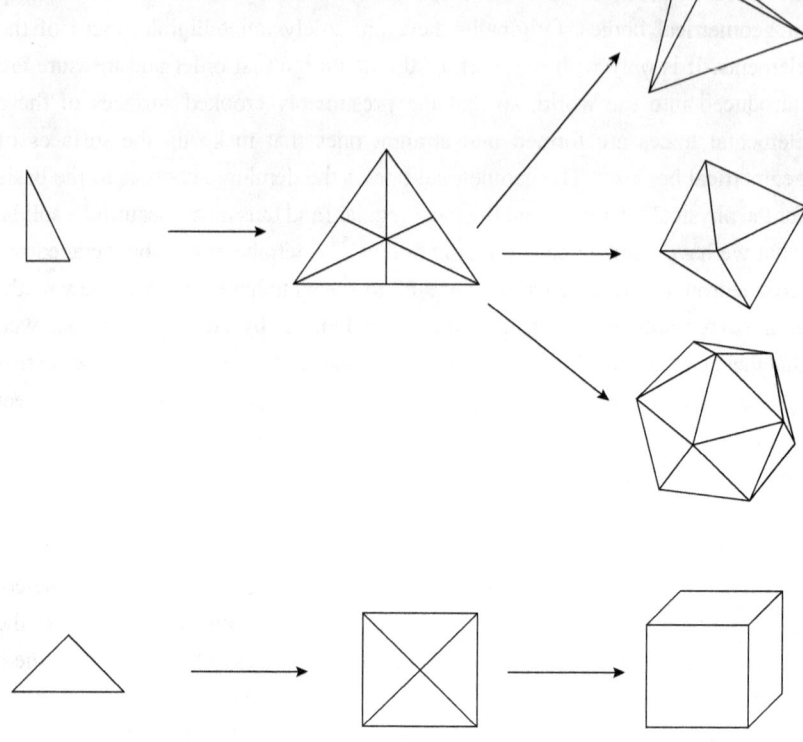

Figure 2 Platonic solids made out of basic triangles.[60]

constituting fire have a tendency to move to other pieces of fire and are connected to the Form of fire in that they are an image of that Form (51b–52a).

Like mathematical solids, these building blocks of the elements can also be transformed into each other. The transformation rules follow their mathematical base: thus a particle of air can dissolve into two particles of fire, since an octahedron provides the surfaces required to build two tetrahedra out of it.

While the Plato of the *Republic* is concerned about the intelligible status of mathematical objects, in the *Timaeus* we find Plato focused on the usage of geometrical figures for the explanation of the universe. He does not discuss the ontological status of the geometrical solids, but we have also no reason to assume he has given up on his earlier idea of 'the square itself' (*Republic* 510d–e), only because he is dealing with many squares in the physical world. For him, the many geometrical solids are used to make the world understandable – and literally so, since they (and not just an approximation to them) are the

---

[60] Adapted from Restrepo and Villaveces (2012).

Philosophy of Mathematics from the Pythagoreans to Euclid   21

constituents of the physical elements. They can keep their non-perceptible status due to the fact that they are too small for perception and the many geometrical solids that together form a phenomenon appear not as geometrical solids, but as physical elements.

This 'geometrical atomism'[61] allows Plato to tie the plurality and changeability of the phenomenal world to intelligible mathematical structures. He traces physical and perceptual features, like the piercing experience of the heat of fire, back to mathematical ones, like the acuteness of the angles of the tetrahedra constituting fire (*Timaeus* 61d–62a). This mathematisation of the universe, however, also shows that the physical realm cannot be assimilated to the mathematical realm without further ado. Plato's attempt to do so leads to at least three problems: first, for reasons of regularity and exhaustiveness, Plato assumes the Platonic solids to be the basis of the elements – but there are five Platonic solids, and only four physical elements in ancient physics; so the mathematical basis does not fit exactly the physical requirements. Plato is aware of this problem and accordingly gives an account of what happens to the fifth geometrical element eventually: the dodecahedron is assumed to be the form of the world as a whole (55c), as it seems to be close enough to a sphere, which was assumed as a form for the world body before because of its regularity and completeness (33b). Second, while Timaeus himself suggests that on the phenomenal level, it appears as if all four elements can be transformed into each other (49b–c), the mathematical basis in fact excludes earth from such transformations since cubes are made of a different kind of triangles than tetrahedra, octahedra, and icosahedra (54b–d).

In these two cases we see that the underlying geometrical structure leads to assumptions that are in tension with phenomenal observations or physical needs. By contrast, the third problem is a consequence from the mathematical realm that is in need of further explanation in the *Timaeus*: while the elemental changes between fire, air, and water are accounted for in terms of the number of faces (so that, for example, two tetrahedra which turn into one octahedron do indeed share the same number of faces), what is problematic are the changes of the volumes resulting from such an elemental change; for the volume of the two tetrahedra is only half the volume of the octahedron. Given that Plato excludes any void between the elements (58a, 59a), and elemental change is a constant feature of the universe, an explanation would be needed why these continuous elemental transformations do not lead to incessant changes of volumes of the universe.[62]

---

[61] Atomism here implies that there is a distinction between what truly is, the geometrical bodies in this case, and what appears – here, fire, air, etc.

[62] Moreover, Aristotle in *Metaphysics* M, 2, 1076b objects that the Platonist position will lead to ontological inflation: if there are separate mathematical solids, there will be separate mathematical planes, lines, points, etc.

Furthermore, the transfer of mathematical features to the physical realm raises the question whether the consequences these mathematical features bring with them should be dealt with as they are in mathematics or not – for example, should we assume that three-dimensional bodies can be made up of planes, as they are in mathematics? Aristotle answers with a clear no, Plato with a clear yes. Plato makes the physical realm fit the mathematical and assumes mathematical rules to be valid for the physical world, a view which Aristotle contests.

1.4 Mathematical Objects as Abstractions in Aristotle

Aristotle develops a third position concerning the ontology of mathematical objects. While he does not give us a treatise laying out in detail his own position, we can reconstruct it from his refutation of positions that assume independently existing mathematical entities in *Metaphysics* M.

In contrast to Plato's assumption that mathematics deals with independently and separately existing objects, for Aristotle mathematics deals with perceptible things, since they are the only things that exist for him. However, mathematicians do not deal with these sensible objects insofar as they are perceptible, for example, insofar as they have colours and are made from a certain material, but insofar as they have mathematically relevant properties, for example, extensions such as length. While the fact that a certain building, like the Palazzo Vecchio, has a square façade is accidental to its being a government building (it would also work as a government building if the façade was a rectangle), it is what the mathematician will take as object of investigation. And since it is the best way to investigate what really interests her, the mathematician will treat this feature accidental to the building as if it were separate (from its material, etc.). She thus posits what is accidental as independently existing and makes her object of investigation independent of the changes the physical thing may undergo (or its generation and corruption).[63]

Aristotle's position has three aspects – abstraction, being separate in thought, and what is called a 'qua-operator'. Let us briefly look at each of these.

Qua-operator: this operator is a tool commonly used by Aristotle but especially important for his account of mathematics. It makes it clear that we are looking at some x *insofar as* it is y, that is, *qua* y.[64] And insofar as x is y, only certain properties are relevant (usually a sub-set of the properties of x). For example, an arithmetician looks at a turtle *qua* one indivisible unit (insofar as

---

[63] For we need mathematical objects to be eternal and unchanging.

[64] Lear (1982) understands it as a filter that filters out what is inessential to the discussion and thus isolates the relevant logical space. See also Annas (1987) and Mendell (2004).

turtles can be considered as such units, they can be counted) and a geometer can look at the same turtle *qua* a solid (insofar as the turtle is, for example, shaped like a spherical segment, it will have the properties suitable for such spherical segments). Two understandings of the qua-locution have been suggested within Aristotelian scholarship: as looking at one specific aspect or property or as indicating a specific approach to the subject.

Being separated in thought: with the help of the qua-operator, the mathematicians can posit the mathematical object as separate in their thinking.[65] This means that the mathematical object can be defined without referring to that from which it was abstracted (for example, the features of a sphere can be investigated without any reference to the physical ball from which the sphere was abstracted). For Aristotle, only substances can exist independently, but not quantities (which is what he regards mathematical objects to be) nor any of the features he considers as belonging to the other categories (such as qualities). Nevertheless, for all mathematical purposes, mathematical objects can be treated as if they were separate – separate from the substances they were abstracted from as well as from the motions and changes of these substances. Metaphysically, however, the basic things there are, are still substances, which are the only things that can in fact exist separately on their own for Aristotle. Treating mathematical objects as if they were separate when they really are not, has been seen as a mere façon de parler; or even as a form of fictionalism on Aristotle's part.[66]

Abstraction: The starting point for Aristotle is the perceptible thing, from which we then abstract certain features. This abstraction is, however, not any old lack of attention to certain features that the mathematicians perform, but an *intended inattentiveness*[67] – anything that is not of mathematical interest is disregarded; we only attend to certain features and intentionally leave out others.[68]

This still leaves it open, however, what exactly we take the things to be that we abstract from and what we take the result of the abstraction to be. Are we disregarding the matter of a physical thing or are we disregarding certain features, such as possessing colour or being moved? And is the result a certain object, for example, a square, or is it certain properties, such as extension or roundness? What about those mathematical features that do not seem to be

---

[65] 'Positing' here does not mean stipulating something that is not there, but rather seeing something as its own object of investigation which we encounter in the sensible world as part of a compound.

[66] So Mendell (2004). On the other hand, Aristotle claims that mathematical things really exist, for things either exist, as he says, 'in actuality or as matter (i.e. potentially)', and he seems to think of mathematical things to exist potentially, in the way a statue exists in a block of marble.

[67] See Annas (1987).

[68] Lang (2021) calls his position that mathematics deals with abstract mathematical properties, and not with abstract objects which are possessed by physical systems, that of an 'Aristotelian realist'.

instantiated (for example, a particular angle)? And how can abstraction work in the case of counting – can we really abstract away everything from a thing apart from the fact that it is one thing in order to gain a unit? Or is all we need in this case an appropriate sortal?

These points lead to two bigger questions – (a) is abstraction for Aristotle one unified process and (b) does it require some form of idealisation? (a) Do we in all cases abstract from the same kind of things in the same kind of process or does abstraction mean different things in different instances? The understanding of abstraction seems to differ with different cases, for example, if I count the turtles in the zoo, I seem to undertake a different kind of abstraction than if I abstract from the physical features of my turtle so as to derive a spherical segment. But if it is not always the same kind of process, how then do we know what is the right thing to abstract from in each case? Is it enough if this is decided by the person counting or abstracting? (b) Idealisation may be seen as required at two possible points in Aristotle's account: on the one hand we may think that in order to derive a tangent that does indeed touch the circle at only one point or a triangle whose angles do indeed equal 180 degrees, it is not enough to abstract from matter and other properties of physical circles and triangles, but we may also have to idealise the slightly crooked lines to derive straight lines or perfectly curved ones and the mathematical properties mathematicians do indeed study.[69] Furthermore, there may be cases where in fact no instantiation does indeed exist even though we can construct them mathematically.[70] In both cases it would seem mathematicians may also have to add something to the physical world (a section of the straight line, for example, or the angle not instantiated in the world). But if the mathematician and thus her mind 'adds' something, is the thus gained triangle not mind-dependent? Accordingly, with respect to the ontological status of mathematical things, Aristotle's account of mathematical objects has sometimes been understood as a version of psychologism, and mathematics as subjective (which would make the applicability of mathematical theorems to the natural world problematic and may call into question the position of mathematics as a model science).

Recent scholarship on Aristotle, however, as well as Neoplatonists, have pointed out that Aristotle nowhere claims mathematical objects to be mind-dependent.[71] And the Greek origin of our word 'abstraction', *aphairesis*, which Aristotle for the first time uses in a technical sense, literally means 'taking away'.[72] Accordingly, several scholars have suggested that with Aristotle we

---

[69] Mendell (2004) calls this the 'precision problem'. He does not think Aristotle ever explains his solution to this problem.
[70] Similarly, Hussey (1993) has pointed out that according to Aristotle there are not infinitely many actual straight lines in the world but infinitely many in mathematics.
[71] See Mendell (2004) and Proclus (1992), 12.10–16.   [72] See Cleary (1985).

should talk about subtraction rather than abstraction – for him everything is there already with the sensible things, certain features just have to be subtracted; there is no addition that an idealisation seems to suggest. For Aristotle, what mathematicians do is not to create something, but rather to actualize what exists already potentially (the line has the potential to be lengthened and its crookedness to be disregarded).[73]

Summing up, we can say that mathematical objects are not independently existing objects for Aristotle, rather they depend on the sensible objects we perceive; they are features of these objects that we separate in thought, but they do not depend on our mind for their existence. It may seem ironic then that Aristotle, for whom the objects of mathematics are much closer to sensible objects than for Plato, is very cautious to make it clear that the construction principles of mathematics, such as that from lines and surfaces we can construct solids, do not hold for physical bodies which Plato in his *Timaeus* seems to assume.

2 Epistemology: Mathematical Knowledge versus Philosophical Knowledge

In this chapter we will look at different accounts of the relationship between mathematical and philosophical knowledge and at the epistemological status of basic propositions and deductive procedures. In the last chapter, with Philolaus, we saw the idea that mathematical structures may be seen as a necessary condition for knowledge, though it remained underdetermined what kind of knowledge he had in mind. In Plato's *Meno* and in Aristotle's *Posterior Analytics* mathematical knowledge seems to be used as a model for scientific knowledge – the claim to completeness and perfect veracity and its method of demonstration make especially geometry a paradigmatic example of a science for philosophers. The mathematical sciences were one of the few already established sciences outside of philosophy and probably the most prominent and exact among them, so using them as models for scientific knowledge may have seemed rather natural. In Plato's *Republic*, however, mathematical knowledge, while important and central for the education of the future leaders of the state, is clearly distinguished from the highest form of philosophical knowledge, namely dialectic, which is meant to work with non-hypothetical starting points. Finally, we will also consider the role of explanations in ancient mathematics according to Aristotle.

---

[73] What we may miss in order to account for mathematical objects not instantiated in the physical realm, is an explicit claim that some abstractions can be combined to form different mathematical objects (an idea that we are used to from similar discussions in early modern times).

2.1 Mathematical Knowledge as a Model

Plato frequently uses the mathematical sciences as examples for secure knowledge or exact sciences.[74] In his *Meno* mathematical knowledge seems to be employed as a model of real knowledge that we do not derive from the world but bring already with us.[75] We find two passages there that use geometry as a paradigm for knowledge and inquiry, respectively. The first one (82b–86b) is better known and shows a young Greek slave coming to find a solution to the problem of how to double the area of a given square without any prior geometrical knowledge. Plato introduces it as a reaction to the so-called Meno Paradox (also called Paradox of Inquiry), the problem raised by Meno that inquiry seems to be impossible or useless: if we do not know beforehand what we inquire, inquiry seems to be impossible as (a) we will not know what to look for when starting our inquiry and (b) we will not recognise it once we have stumbled upon it. And if we do already know what we are looking for, inquiry seems unnecessary.

As a response to this seeming paradox, Plato wants to show that we do indeed already possess knowledge of what we learn beforehand, but we have forgotten and need to be reminded of it. Accordingly, his so-called theory of recollection claims that our inquiries do in fact not produce new knowledge but rather reawaken what we already know in some way; we become aware of knowledge we already possess. The kind of knowledge Plato seems to have in mind (or at least for which his theory seems most plausible) is what we would call a priori knowledge.[76] And the example he gives for such rekindled knowledge is an instance of the geometrical doubling of the area of a square: a young boy who has not been taught any geometry is given a square with an area of four square feet, thus the length of each side being two feet. He is asked to find the length of the side of a square that is double this area, so eight feet. Not having any experience in mathematics, he first tries a square with double the length of the sides and then using sides of three feet length. Eventually, Socrates brings out the right answer from him with the help of a diagram: a square with an area of eight feet has a side with the length of the diagonal of the two feet square (see figure 3). This mathematical example is meant to show how somebody without experience or training can derive new knowledge simply by deduction.

---

[74] For example, in *Gorgias* 451a–c or *Protagoras* 356d–357a.
[75] At least this is what the back reference to the *Meno* in Plato's *Phaedo* suggests when it is claimed that the ability to remember correctly if questioned in the right way (which for Plato is the way to acquire knowledge) 'is shown most clearly if you lead them to diagrams', i.e. to geometrical reasoning (73b).
[76] For Plato, it is a certain content of knowledge, rather than an ability or capability of reasoning that we already possess.

Philosophy of Mathematics from the Pythagoreans to Euclid 27

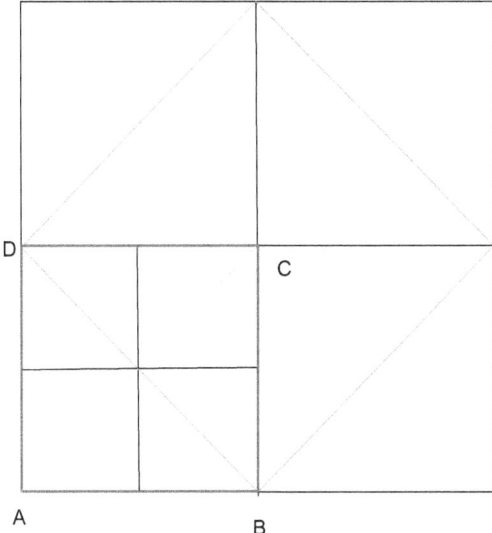

Figure 3 Doubling the area of a square in the *Meno*.

In this geometrical example, we can look at the diagram of the square ABCD and its diagonals and from this 'see' how to proceed. We acquire geometrical knowledge via seeing the figure of the original square that is divided by the diagonals so that we then can 'count the triangles' constituting the squares without, however, depending on this particular drawing (we could as well simply imagine one in our head). There seem to be a couple of problems, however, with this example: for instance, we are explicitly told at the end that the young boy ends up with true opinion, not yet knowledge (85c); we seem to begin with an arithmetical question (how long is the side of a square with double the area of the two-feet square), but end up with the boy simply pointing to the line of the diagonal; and Socrates' leading questions have been seen as in fact doing much more than simply help the boy discover the knowledge already within himself.[77] All these objections, however, do not undermine the fact that Plato uses a mathematical example as a paradigm for knowledge that can be derived a priori. Socrates' questions may be leading questions that prompt certain answers, but his careful layout of steps leading to the solution of the problem ends up showing the boy's ability to follow a deduction or a kind of proof.[78] And while the boy ends up pointing to a line, this move from what seems to be an arithmetical question to a geometrical answer (the

---

[77] E.g., are the two diagonals, which Socrates introduces, not a necessary pointer for the slave boy? For their lines cut up the original small square into equal parts and thus the slave boy can count the parts inside and is pushed in the direction of dividing up the original square.

[78] See Scott (2006), chapter 9. Knorr (1975) even suggests that what we find in the *Meno* is what a Pythagorean proof for the incommensurability may have looked like.

length of the diagonal of the original square) simply mirrors the fact that the answer to this question has to be geometrical within the context of Greek mathematics. For the problem of doubling the square has a geometrical solution (i.e. the diagonal) in ancient mathematics, but no arithmetical one, since we cannot arrive at the side of the square in question numerically within the realm of positive integers.[79] But the task of finding a square of double the area is nevertheless achieved: Socrates is satisfied when they have reached the new square (without any indication of irony here), and Meno and Socrates do not have to discuss first whether this is an instance of knowledge. That the boy is seen as ending up with true opinion rather than knowledge is explicitly claimed to rest on the fact that the insight gained is not yet tied down in his mind (85c), but frequent questioning will tie it down and thus turn it from true opinion to knowledge.[80]

While we are not given a general view of Plato's account of mathematics here, it is remarkable that he uses this geometrical piece of reasoning as the prominent example of recollection in the *Meno* and the *Phaedo* and lets it serve as a paradigm for something that is indisputably knowledge (it is knowledge which Meno and Socrates themselves possess, so they can clearly see when the boy goes wrong and when he has reached the right answer). The geometrical construction allows him to show the process of inquiry and it provides the security that we are doubtlessly dealing with a piece of knowledge,[81] since the mathematicians agree on the fact that we gain a square with double the area from building it on the diagonal of the original square; an agreement that may be much harder to reach on philosophical questions.

In the second geometrical passage, 86c–87b, we are presented with a mathematical method that is used as a model for philosophical investigation, the hypothetical method.[82] The idea is that with problems we cannot solve straightaway, we may nevertheless make progress by spelling out possible consequences for the different possible solutions. So while we may not be able to give an answer to a particular problem, we may nevertheless say that if it is x, then y follows and if it is w then z follows. For the issue at hand in the *Meno*, this

---

[79] Socrates seems to hint at the problem of incommensurability between the diagonal and the side of the square when he tells the boy 'to show' the side of the double square 'if he cannot calculate it' (84a); see Knorr (1975), p. 26 and chapter 3.

[80] We seem to deal with a different account of knowledge here than in the *Republic*, where knowledge is set over a different realm than opinion is (the former over the intelligible, the latter over the perceptible), while here in the *Meno* we can have both opinion as well as knowledge about mathematical things and the way to Larissa. This difference in the account of knowledge may also be part of the reason for the different view of the relationship between mathematical and philosophical knowledge Plato seems to present in the *Meno* and the *Republic*.

[81] A security presumably needed by Plato as a basis to introduce his new concept of recollection.

[82] The Platonic text explicitly links this examination 'from hypothesis' to what geometers do. For understanding it as the mathematical method of analysis, see Menn (2002), p. 212.

Philosophy of Mathematics from the Pythagoreans to Euclid 29

means that whereas it does not seem possible to answer the question directly whether virtue is teachable, it is possible to say that if it is knowledge, then it is indeed teachable, but if it is not knowledge it may not be. While this method does not as such lead to answer the question whether virtue is teachable in the *Meno* – for this Meno and Socrates would first have to inquire into what virtue is and attempt to find a definition[83] – it presents a way forward and a method of discovery.

Both geometrical passages are used for the overall interest of Plato's dialogue in ethical knowledge, the question what virtue is and whether it is teachable. Geometrical knowledge is introduced in order to show how acquiring knowledge in general is possible and how to deal with questions that do not seem to be answerable directly. And these passages may be seen as suggesting that geometry and philosophy are similarly deductive.[84] Thus these passages have been read by some as the first inkling of the idea that philosophy can work 'in a geometrical manner', *more geometrico*; the most literal and extensive understanding of this we probably find in Spinoza's *Ethics Demonstrated in Geometrical Order*.[85]

Let us now move on to Aristotle's *Posterior Analytics*, his theory of demonstration and account of how to organize and present the results of research as a systematic science.[86] For this, Aristotle uses the mathematical sciences to provide him with crucial and often the most prominent examples; and it is evident that the mathematical sciences are not only a very clear case of scientific knowledge, but in many respects a model for him.[87] While it has been argued that the model of a science Aristotle works with is in fact not mathematics, but biology,[88] the two seem to be models in very different senses: biology is a model science for Aristotle in the sense that he wants to establish such a science in his own work, but it is not yet such a science when Aristotle enters the philosophical scene; rather, it becomes such a science only with him.[89] By contrast, the mathematical sciences are already existing sciences that his audience would

---

[83] Without clarifying first what virtue is, the two are led to what seem to be opposing conclusions about the possibility of teaching virtue; this is, however, not due to the method as such, but rather to the fact that without this clarification Socrates and Meno seem to find support for understanding virtue as knowledge as well as not as knowledge.

[84] See Broadie (2021), p. 191.

[85] In early modern times, this style was seen as taking up the methodical way we find in Euclid's *Elements*.

[86] See also Section 3.   [87] See also Cleary (1985), p. 18.

[88] See, for example, Lenox (2021), who points out that Aristotle's *History of Animals* 491a7–14 suggests that his biological project is organized in accordance with the theory of the *Posterior Analytics*. And in general, Aristotle's own biology has been seen as fitting the model of demonstrative knowledge of the *Posterior Analytics* very closely.

[89] Which also Lennox (2021) seems to admit when he speaks about biology being a science only from Aristotle *onwards*.

be familiar with.⁹⁰ And we should not forget that the mathematical sciences were one of the few already established sciences outside of philosophy and probably the most rigorous among them. Aristotle can draw from the mathematical sciences in order to show to his audience, for example, the role principles play, the classification of principles, and, more generally, the way a deductive science works; they are a model he can refer to for how a science should be organized and set out.⁹¹ This does not necessarily mean mathematics is a science that philosophy should emulate in its form (given that geometry works with constructions, this does not even seem possible), but in its systematicity and rigor.

At the very beginning of his *Posterior Analytics*, Aristotle takes up the idea from the *Meno* that learning requires prior knowledge: 'All teaching and all learning of an intellectual kind proceed from pre-existent knowledge' (71a1f.). Talking about 'intellectual learning' here, Aristotle makes room for knowledge by perception, while Plato talks about knowledge full stop.⁹² For Aristotle, there are two ways in which we must already have knowledge at the beginning of an inquiry: of some things we must already believe *that* they are, of others we must grasp *what* the things spoken about are. The examples he gives for these kinds of prior knowledge are, as with Plato, mathematical, but also logical:

> For example, of the fact that everything is either asserted or denied truly, we must believe that it is the case; of the triangle, that it means this; and of the unit both (both what it means and that it is) (71a13–16).

We see that Aristotle first gives a logical example – of the principle of the excluded middle we must know that it holds, in such a way that everything is either asserted or denied. And then he switches to two mathematical examples: of a triangle we must know what it means (but not that it exists, since it is not the most basic element of geometry and its existence can be proven by construction). And of the unit we must both know what it means and that it is since it is the most basic item in arithmetic, namely the element of numbers. For Aristotle, too, there must be some form of knowledge prior to any teaching and learning. Mathematical knowledge and logical principles, such as those referred to in the passage just quoted, demonstrate this. For Aristotle, we know certain things universally before we learn, but we do not know them simpliciter. As an

---

⁹⁰ Furthermore, it has often been claimed that at least a good part of Aristotle's *Analytics* was already written while he was still a member of the Academy (see Barnes (1993), p. xiv), while he seems to have started his mature biological work only after he had left Athens and had moved to Lesbos (see Balme (1987), p. 13, though he claims this especially for the *History of Animals*).
⁹¹ See Mendell (2004), §2: Aristotle's discussions on the best format for a deductive science in the *Posterior Analytics* reflect the practice of contemporary mathematics as taught and practiced in Plato's Academy; see also McKirahan (1992), p. 133.
⁹² In the *Republic* 'perceptual knowledge' would not count as knowledge for Plato, but as opinion.

example for knowing something universally but not simpliciter he gives us a mathematical example concerning triangles: 'you already knew that every triangle has angles equal to two right-angles; but you got to know that this figure in the semicircle is a triangle at the same time as you were being led to the conclusion' (71a19–21).

Both Plato and Aristotle use mathematics for showing that we do not get into Meno's paradox. In *Metaphysics* 1025b4–7, Aristotle uses mathematics and medicine as examples with the help of which he generalizes his inferences for all sciences. And in *De caelo* 306a23 ff. he attacks certain atomistic accounts by claiming they assert that not all bodies are divisible and thus come into conflict with 'our most accurate sciences, namely the mathematical'.

2.2 The Distinction between Mathematical Knowledge and the Highest Form of Philosophical Knowledge in Plato

While at least in some texts Plato and Aristotle understand mathematics as potentially an ideal science, this does not mean, however, that the two do not also sometimes criticise mathematics as it is practised at their time for falling short of such a science.[93] And in his *Republic* Plato makes it clear that mathematics is not the highest form of knowledge. The mathematical sciences are very important to turn the soul towards the intelligibles there, but the philosophical discipline of dialectic, which deals with the first principles of what there is, is seen as a more fundamental science.

This is probably made most explicit in Plato's so-called example of the line, which is part of a series of three well-known examples in the *Republic* to explain what is and can be known – the example of the sun, of the line, and of the cave. The line example shows a fourfold division of the realm of what is, as well as of the cognitive states with which we can access these different things; thus it closely links ontology and epistemology.[94] And it places mathematics clearly below dialectics – the lower ontological status of mathematical objects goes hand in hand with a lower epistemological status of mathematical knowledge.

This example asks us to think of a line divided first into two sections – one standing for the visible realm, the other for the intelligible realm (509d8), the first is what is opinable, the second what is knowable. Each of the two sections is then divided again into two sections, so that we end up with four sections in total (see Figure 4).[95] Of the visible realm, we are given objects first: to the first

---

[93] See also Section 3. [94] At least on many interpretations of the line.
[95] They are explicitly said to be four unequal sections – how exactly to understand these differences in length of the individual sections is a matter of dispute in the literature; see Broadie (2021). I have used one interpretation for the drawing here – letting the length of the line segment correspond

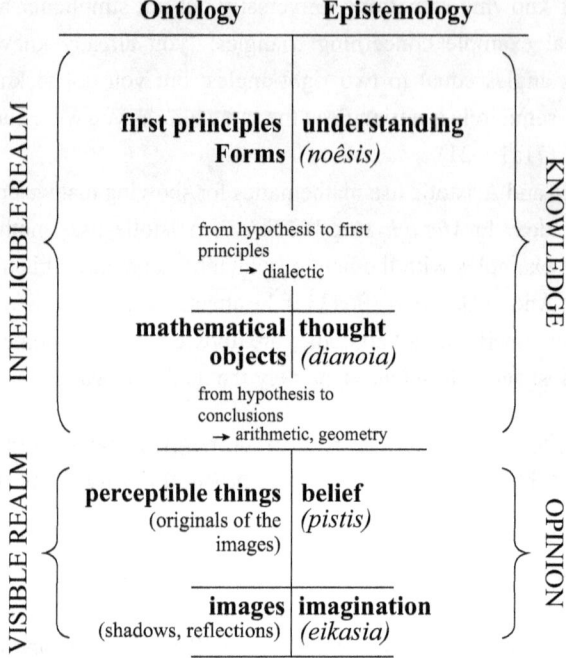

Figure 4 The divided line in Plato's *Republic*.

subsection belong all kinds of images, such as shadows and reflections in water; while to the second subsection belong all the originals of these images, that is, perceptible living things as well as artificial ones. Of the intelligible realm, the first section uses the originals of the visible world as images (in the way we use a diagram in geometry or a bronzen sphere as a visualisation of a sphere as such) and proceeds from hypothesis to conclusions; while in the second and last sub-section we proceed from hypothesis to first principles without using images; this is the realm of first principles and Forms. These two sections of the intelligible realm are not characterised by different objects so much as by different methods. In the following, we are told that the people using the method described in the first sub-section of the intelligible realm are those dealing with geometry and arithmetic (510c2–3), and that they use as images the lines they draw. Their claims are, however, not about those lines drawn, but rather about 'the square itself' and 'the diagonal itself' (510d7–8). Of the second-subsection, which goes to unhypothetical first principles, we are told that its

---

directly to the amount of clarity. But the only thing relevant for us is that the ratio of the different sections is in some way done according to the relative amount of clarity and opacity of each section (509d). The four sections display a ratio not only of A:B=C:D, but also of A:C=B:D.

Philosophy of Mathematics from the Pythagoreans to Euclid   33

objects – first principles and Forms – are grasped by dialectic. We access the mathematical things by thought (*dianoia*), but the Forms by understanding (*noêsis*); while belief (*pistis*) is of perceptible things and imagination (*eikasia*) of images (511c5–e4). Understanding and thought together form the realm of knowledge, belief and imagination the realm of opinion.

While the example of the line does not discuss mathematics in any detail, we can derive at least four important points, epistemological as well as ontological ones, from it for our project:

1) The true objects of mathematics are things like 'the square itself' and the 'diagonal itself' – the objects the mathematicians are concerned with do really exist, but only in the intelligible realm, not in the perceptible one. They are what it means to be a square, not this or that particular square.
2) The mathematicians use what is perceptible only as images for the intelligible objects they are really talking about.
3) The way mathematicians proceed is from hypothesis to conclusions without deriving first principles.
4) Since the mathematicians do not turn to first principles, but start from given axioms, their activity is not concerned with the most fundamental things in the way dialectic is.

In the *Republic*, dialectic is understood to be more fundamental than mathematics, since it deals with the first principles of what there is. Mathematics is situated below dialectics because it cannot justify its principles[96] in the way dialectics allegedly can – and perhaps also because geometry relies on the perceptible world for its operations, as when diagrams are used for proofs.[97] This also suggests that dialectic and mathematics do not provide knowledge of the very same type[98] and probably that knowledge of the principles and knowledge of what is derived from principles differ not only in status but also in kind; but Plato says very little here that would allow us to flesh out these epistemological differences in any detail.

While mathematical knowledge is not the highest form of knowledge, it is nevertheless crucial according to the *Republic* in order to turn the soul around, from the perceptible realm to the intelligible one (521d). This turning requires a very long education in mathematics for the future rulers of the state, the so-called philosopher queens and kings of the kallipolis (521c–535a): as small children, they are taught music, poetry, and are engaged in physical exercises; after which a ten-year period of training in different mathematical sciences

---

[96] Resting on axioms that simply have to be assumed.   [97] See Section 3.
[98] Even though mathematics is 'dreaming' of the objects of dialectic, as we will see later.

ensues. In each case the real interest is for the pure version of this branch of mathematics. But in order to show that acquiring these different kinds of mathematical knowledge does not make students useless for practical tasks, the fact that there are applied branches of mathematics is also employed. First, arithmetic is taught; explicitly not for the purpose of commerce (525c–d), but as the basis for order and for all sciences. It is seen to be required for warfare; but most of all in order to lead the philosophical mind to the one and numbers as such and thus to intelligible things. Then geometry is introduced, not just so that the students will be prepared for practical purposes, like setting up a camp or dealing with different formations of an army, but most of all so that its students turn towards what truly is. Within the systematic layout of the sciences, solid geometry – stereometry – would be next, but according to the Socrates of the *Republic* this is a subject that has not really been explored so far. Given that we do find it in Euclid's *Elements*, scholars have suggested that this claim in Plato's middle period represents a time before *Theaetetus* had done his work on the Platonic solids that turn up in Plato's later work, in the *Timaeus*.

With the last two subjects, astronomy and harmonics, Socrates turns to mathematical subjects that are per se practical and thus closer to the perceptible realm. But in the education of the future philosophers, they should be taken up in as pure a form as possible, so that astronomy 'leaves the things in the sky alone' (530b–c). True astronomy should not be done as it is 'currently' practised – that is, as concerned with the visible movements of the heavenly bodies – but as concerned with the intelligible model of what we see in the sky, that is, in the way geometry is.[99] It is a kind of ideal kinematics that is only imperfectly expressed in the visible heavens in time and space (as the irregularities of the motions of the heavenly bodies show, such as the changing ratio of day and night). Similarly, harmonics should not be concerned with the audible tones so much as with the pure mathematics belonging to it (531a–c).

A systematic connection between these mathematical sciences – arithmetic, geometry, astronomy, and harmonics – is already claimed by the Pythagoreans, who call them sister-sciences. But in contrast to the Pythagoreans, Plato's *Republic* is concerned with a pure form of these sciences that deals with the perceptible realm as little as possible and should thus guide the students from the perceptible to the intelligible realm. According to Plato, this path from the perceptible to the intelligible is very difficult for us, and mathematics has the power to lead us along this path. Learning to focus on intelligible things from mathematics is crucial for the ascent to philosophy for the middle Plato.

---

[99] Which should take the visible simply as illustration.

But these mathematical sciences are not the highest sciences in the *Republic*. The coping stone is dialectic. The *Republic* points out that we cannot expect a full account of dialectic here (532e–533a); nor will we get one in the other dialogues of Plato. But the *Republic* makes it clear that dialectic is the journey out of the cave, that is, the process through which we get to understand what each thing is in itself and what the Good itself is, the highest Form of Being. This is done solely by means of argument (*dialegesthai*). The difference between dialectic and mathematics, at least in its pure form that should be used in the education of the guardians, is not so much that the later uses perception, as the example of the line may seem to suggest. But rather their respective treatment of the first principles, which according to Plato is such that dialectic is the only

> inquiry that systematically attempts to grasp with respect to each thing itself what the being of it is, for all the other crafts are concerned with human opinions and desires, with growing or construction, or with the care of growing or constructed things. And as for the rest, I mean geometry and the subjects that follow it, we described them as to some extent grasping what is, for we saw that, while they do dream about what is, they are unable to command a waking view of it as long as they make use of hypotheses that they leave untouched and that they cannot give any account of. What mechanism could possibly turn any agreement into knowledge when it begins with something unknown and puts together the conclusion and the steps in between from what is unknown? (533b–c).

Dialectic is the only systematic knowledge inquiring the being of each thing, while almost all of the other so-called crafts deal with becoming (growing, construction). Mathematics has a special status in that it is at least 'dreaming' of what truly is; but the problem is that the mathematicians start from a hypothesis of which they cannot give an account. Thus they base their discipline on something 'unknown'; while dialectic allegedly gives an account of these first principles. Plato here even goes so far as to claim that this means that the mathematical sciences are not sciences in the strict sense (533c–d); rather, they are something 'clearer than opinion, but darker than knowledge'.

Also other authors have seen mathematics as a kind of essential propaedeutic. Plato's contemporary, the rhetorician Isocrates, for example, recommends mathematics to make children quicker for learning other subjects and in order to get used to the fact that the process of acquiring knowledge demands hard thought and precision.[100] But for Plato, mathematics achieves much more than this by training our mind to deal with the intelligible, instead of the perceptible. And some interpreters, like Burnyeat, have even claimed that mathematical

---

[100] Isocrates 15 (*Antidosis*), 265; cf. also Heath (1921), p. 21.

structures for Plato are 'a constitutive part of ethical understanding',[101] which includes at least two ideas: first, central concepts of the mathematical sciences, such as unity, proportion, and concord, are also central for the political realm so that the structures studied in mathematics 'are the very structures that the philosopher-rulers will seek to establish in the social order of the ideal city and in the souls of its citizens'. And second, since mathematical theorems are unqualifiedly true in every context, which is what Plato wants to show for the realm of ethical value, it articulates objective values.

Let us finally look at the kind of explanation mathematics provides according to ancient philosophers.

2.3 The Possibility of Explanation in the Mathematical Sciences

In contemporary philosophy of mathematics, one central epistemological question concerns the possibility of explanations in mathematics. More exactly speaking, it is debated whether we find within mathematics (a) real explanations (and not just non-explanatory demonstrations) and (b) explanations for the sciences.[102] We seem to get into similar worries if we look at Aristotle's account of scientific understanding that closely ties knowledge to causes, as we can see from the following passage:

> We think we know a thing simpliciter (and not in the sophistic fashion accidentally) when we think we understand both that the cause (*aitia*), because of which the object is, is its cause, and that it is not possible for this to be otherwise. (*Post. An.* I, 1, 71b9–12)

We see that knowledge is defined as understanding the cause of a thing to be this cause and to be necessarily this cause. So there are two conditions for understanding something simpliciter, (a) knowing the cause and (b) this being tied to some form of necessity.[103] Given that knowledge and understanding is tied to causes here,[104] we may be worried that such an account does not fit mathematics at all, as causes seem to belong to the area of the natural sciences only. How can mathematics explain anything if knowledge and understanding is of causes for Aristotle?[105]

---

[101] Burnyeat (2000). By contrast, according to Broadie (2021) the future rulers need these ten years of mathematical training because it is so hard to turn away from the perceptible to the intelligible realm for us.
[102] See Mancosu et al. (2023) for a discussion.
[103] The necessity can either be taken to indicate that 'a understands X only if X cannot be otherwise' or as 'a understands X only if a knows that X cannot be otherwise'.
[104] E.g., we understand a lunar eclipse for Aristotle if we know the cause of its coming about (we know that the interposition of the earth leads to a deprivation of light from the moon; 90a).
[105] Compare already Proclus (1992), 158–159. Proclus as well as Simplicius claim that for Aristotle mathematics is not an explanatory science; see also Harari (2008).

First we need to point out that the Greek word usually translated as 'causes', *aitia*, is much broader than our usual understanding of a cause. For Aristotle, *aitia* are not only efficient causes, but explicitly include formal, material, and teleological causes, as he makes clear in *Physics* II, 3; they are better understood as reasons or 'becauses'. Accordingly, Barnes (1993) translates them as 'explanations' rather than 'causes'. Aristotle's main point here is that knowledge includes having a grasp of why something is the case.[106]

Aristotle claims that arithmetic, geometry, and optics carry out their demonstrations through what he calls the first figure in his syllogistic, which he takes to be especially scientific, and belong to the sciences that inquire into the reason why (*Posterior Analytics* I, 14, 79a17–24). Accordingly, he assumes that there is some explanation within mathematics itself.[107] But does mathematics also provide explanations for the sciences? Here we need to remember that at the time in question, physics and the natural sciences were not mathematicised in the way they are today. However, Aristotle himself introduces mathematical concepts into the realm of physics in order to develop central concepts further.[108] And that mathematics can provide knowledge of 'becauses' in the sciences for Aristotle, he makes clear with examples like the wound in his *Posterior Analytics* (79a14–16): 'it is for the doctors to know the facts that curved wounds heal more slowly, and for the geometers to know the reason why'.[109]

While the doctor will know that a round wound will take longer to heal, a mathematician can explain the reason behind this, presumably, because a round-shaped wound has the biggest surface in relation to its circumference.

So mathematicians can know the reasons why and thus provide explanations also for more empirical sciences. But what makes mathematics a model of a science is its employment of deductions. While deductive structures are first found paradigmatically in mathematics, it is philosophers who then raise questions about the workings of deductions and develop the notion of deductions. As we will see in the next section, it is especially completeness and universality where philosophers started to question the exact workings of the deductive

---

[106] Harari (2008) argues that the explicit question whether we find explanations in mathematics rests on a conceptual shift in later antiquity leading to a restriction of the understanding of causes to what actively brings about an effect. Since according to Aristotle, mathematical objects are not substances in the strict sense and thus cannot actively bring about effects, it seemed to the later ancient tradition that mathematics is not an explanatory science.

[107] We leave it to the side here whether he and we would make the distinction between explanatory and non-explanatory demonstrations in the same way.

[108] Most prominently continuity; see Section 4.2

[109] As for applied sciences, we are told that 'it is for the empirical scientist to know the fact and for the mathematician to know the reason why; for the latter have the demonstrations of the explanations', *Post. An.* I, 13, 79a2–4. So here the applied science establishes the fact but it is pure mathematics which with its demonstration establishes the cause or the reason why; see also Harari (2008), p. 147.

systems they gained from mathematicians. But they also asked more general questions, for example, what can be used as starting points for our deductions; what guarantees that truth is indeed preserved in such a deduction; what does their validity rest on; or whether the principle of non-contradiction is the only essential law for such deductions.[110] The mathematicians, by contrast, seem to take these features of deductions for granted; we do not find any meta-reflections on deductions in Euclid or earlier texts.

Philosophers also ask for reasons why deductibility works at all. For Aristotle, deductibility rests on the form of the system. For him, a deduction allows that from some premises a conclusion containing new information can be derived by necessity and nothing external has to be relied upon for the necessity to hold.[111] The validity of the conclusion simply rests on the very form of the deduction. If we have two premises of the form 'all As are Bs' and 'all Bs are Cs', the inference that 'all As are Cs' is valid, no matter what the content.[112] It is this independence from any concrete empirical content that makes deductive structures so central not only for mathematics, but also for logic. And it is in Aristotle's logic that the basic working of deductions as we find it in mathematics is first explicitly investigated. So, it is to the role of deductions that we will now turn in the next section.

3 Methodology

This section is interested in mathematical methods that were of interest for philosophers. This encompasses methods for making new discoveries,[113] as well as for structuring already acquired bodies of knowledge. Most prominently, mathematical deductions were seen as paradigmatic for philosophical proofs. After having looked at deductions in general, this section will look at one method in particular, namely the development of reductio ad absurdum proofs as an example which was equally fruitful in mathematics and philosophy. For a fuller picture, we would have to look also at methodological innovations in dialectics and the sophistic movement, but we will not have space to do so here.[114]

3.1 Mathematical Deductions as Paradigmatic for Philosophical Proofs

Ancient philosophers took mathematics as a paradigm for a strict demonstrative science, as may best be seen from Aristotle's *Posterior Analytics*, which is the first attempt in Western thought to give an account of the way in which scientific

---

[110] See Knorr (1975), p. 4.   [111] See Section 3.
[112] The truth of the conclusion is simply a function of the system.
[113] The second geometrical passage in the *Meno* already gave us a taste of this.
[114] See Szabo (2004) and Mueller (1969).

results should be structured, organized into an intelligible whole, and presented. According to the *Posterior Analytics*, sciences should be properly expounded in deductive systems.[115] That is, the body of truth of each science should be exhibited as a sequence of theorems derived from a few postulates or axioms. The axiomatisation is to be formalised in the sense that it is formulated in a well-defined language, and its arguments should proceed according to a set of logical rules.[116] Today it is sometimes discussed whether mathematics is a science – in case the natural sciences are taken as paradigm and the lack of dealing with empirical evidence is held against mathematics being a science in this sense. But if we think of science as a systematic body of knowledge, mathematics can not only be seen as a paradigm for this, but also was the first developed science in Western thought. Accordingly, when Aristotle discusses how to structure and systematize knowledge as a science in his *Posterior Analytics*, he uses mathematical sciences as crucial examples.[117] Aristotle, who lived presumably roughly fifty years before Euclid, also provides us with a glimpse of the extent to which the idea of an axiomatized science had already been sketched by mathematicians before Euclid.[118]

Two points are especially important for an axiomatised science: the principles or axioms which serve as starting points for proofs and the rules of deduction. We will deal with the starting points in Section 4, and with the rules of deduction here.

3.1.1 Rules of Deductions

Mathematics could be seen as paradigmatically displaying a deductive structure – both within a single proof and in the way in which the genre of mathematical *Elements* sets out the whole of mathematical knowledge in such a way that each proposition only builds on the basic principles and the preceding propositions (but not on succeeding ones). We can see the deductive structure in mathematics in several propositions in Euclid already from the surface grammar which give a general conditional along the following lines: 'if x (and y), then z has to hold'.[119] So from a given starting point it is shown that something else follows

---

[115] Something we do not find in Babylon and Egypt; see von Fritz (1955), pp. 13–14.
[116] In *Posterior Analytics* I, 12 Aristotle points out that paralogisms are rare in mathematics, since they depend on ambiguity in the middle terms, and ambiguities are easily detectable in mathematics. Mathematics uses what in informal talk we can understand as a well-formulated language.
[117] Aristotle also uses other sciences, such as medicine and biology; but the mathematical sciences are the most important examples for already existing sciences displaying the deductive systems he is interested in.
[118] See Heath (1921), pp. 338–341 for mathematical proofs in Aristotle that we do not find in Euclid.
[119] See, e.g., I, 4, 6, or 8. For a detailed contrast with modern standards of deduction, see Mueller (1969), p. 297.

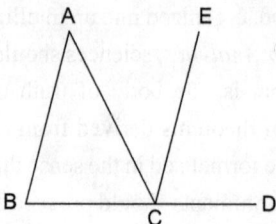

Figure 5 Euclid, *Elements* I, 32.

necessarily. For example, in *Elements* I, 32 we find the following: 'In any triangle, if one of the sides is produced, then the exterior angle equals the sum of the two interior and opposite angles, and the sum of the three interior angles of the triangle equals two right angles.'[120] So here the premises we start out with is that we have a triangle *ABC*, one side of which gets extended (the side *BC* is produced to *D*; see Figure 5). And from this it is then shown that something else follows by necessity, namely that the angle *ACD* equals the sum of the two interior and opposite angles *CAB* and *ABC* and that the sum of the three interior angles *ABC*, *BCA*, and *CAB* equals two right angles. Nothing external comes in here. Solely from what is given and done,[121] prior propositions (I, 13, I, 29, and I, 31), and some basic principles (such as the definition of a triangle), we necessarily derive at what was meant to be shown.

Scholars also talk about 'deductions' with respect to Parmenides' poem, fragment 8, where Parmenides lists the characteristics (*sêmata*) of what truly is, before he 'deduces' them. They are probably the oldest 'deductions' we find in philosophy, and we may think that Aristotle could have looked at Parmenides as a model for deductions.[122] What seems to have made mathematical deductions more attractive than the Parmenidean one for Aristotle are two facts. First, Parmenides' deductions work negatively: by showing that not-F does not fit with what has been established before, they are meant to demonstrate that F has to be true. For example, it is shown that none of the conditions hold that could make what-fundamentally-is inhomogeneous; thus what-fundamentally-is has to be homogeneous.[123] We will talk about a specific form of such indirect proofs later. But for deductions as such, Parmenides' fragments are not a straightforward example. Second, mathematical deductions are

---

[120] Here we do also have the surface grammar being a conditional (*ean*). Often, however, the surface grammar in Greek is not a conditional; and the so-called problems in Euclid's text also have a different structure, such as 'for all x, there can be constructed a *c* such that ... '. Most of the times we can, however, translate Euclid's theorems into such conditionals.

[121] What is done in a construction, when some *a* is applied to some *b*, is also important.

[122] We may also find deductions in the context of rhetoric, sophistry, oratory, and other places, but this is later and less scientific.

[123] For a more detailed account, see Sattler (2019).

used in a systematic way to build a whole science, as we find it in Euclid's *Elements* (and presumably to some extent also in the *Elements* writings available before Euclid). Parmenides's deductions, by contrast, do not so much build a systematic science as give arguments for the different characteristics of what-fundamentally-is. Accordingly, it is no surprise that Aristotle in his *Posterior Analytics* refers to mathematics but not to Parmenides' poem as a model for a deductive method.[124] Hence, we may claim that our philosophical understanding and realisation of deduction was originally shaped by mathematics.

But it is a philosopher, again Aristotle in laying out his logical project, who is the first thinker attempting to define what a deduction is, when in his *Topics* I, 1, 100a25–27 he claims that 'a deduction is an argument in which, certain things being laid down, something other than these necessarily comes about through them.'[125] The word Aristotle uses here for what is translated as 'deduction' is *syllogismos* – and we are dealing with valid and informative deductions in Aristotle. The Greek term *syllogismos* was originally used for reasoning, and in its general form this Aristotelian definition also holds for mathematical inferences. Indeed, it seems that such deductions were first perfected by the mathematicians. Euclid does not talk about *syllogismoi* in his *Elements*, nor does he use the common verb *syllogizesthai*. But in the course of presenting a proof, he commonly uses inferential language – particles expressing consequence,[126] and verbs for inferring or deducing[127] – vocabulary used in ways that indicate what we can characterise as deductions according to Aristotle's definition.

Aristotle's general characterisation of *syllogismos* and his understanding of proofs as demonstrative arguments fits well with the mathematics of his time and Euclid. His narrower understanding of syllogisms, however, is subject to clearly defined restrictions,[128] as his *Analytics* makes clear, that do not hold

---

[124] Even if today we may think from a logical point of view that a mathematical proof is a '(rigorous) *informal proof*', see Horsten (2022).

[125] Aristotle gives almost verbatim the same definition in *Prior Analytics* I.2, 24b18–20. For possible differences between Aristotle's *syllogismoi* and modern deductions, see Barnes (1993), p. 83.

[126] Such as *gar* and *ara*.

[127] Such as *deiknumi* or *epilogizomai*, for example, in X, proposition 62, or *ago* and *sunago* in V, 25 or XIII, 11. Also nouns can express an inferential sense, for example, in X, 4 the Greek word '*porisma*', which is usually translated as 'corollary', makes it clear that what follows is a deduction from a previous demonstration.

[128] Aristotelian syllogisms are inferences with two premises that are categorical propositions, which lead to a categorical proposition as a conclusion. The premises have only one term in common, the so-called middle term, which is either subject or predicate of each premise. The positions of the middle term in each premise lead to different arrangements which Aristotle calls 'figures'. The premise in which the predicate of the conclusion is introduced is called the major premise, the one in which the subject is introduced is called the minor premise.

for mathematics. We also do not find full-blown attempts to reconstruct mathematical proofs syllogistically.[129] This does not mean, however, that mathematics is not a model science for Aristotle. After all, also Aristotle's own natural sciences, his physical and biological works in the way they have come down to us, are not as such presented in syllogistic form. And Aristotle's *Physics* Book Z has been seen as structured according to a mathematical treatise.[130]

Deductive structures as developed in mathematics were seen as a model by philosophers.[131] And we may be tempted to call early Greek geometry and arithmetic not only deductive systems but full-blown axiomatized systems. We should, however, keep in mind that axiomatised systems today are deductively closed and rigorous, like the Peano system. Ancient geometry and arithmetic in the form we know them from Euclid are not complete[132] and not universal to the degree we usually assume: also Euclid's *Elements*, which is a systematic compilation of the mathematical knowledge of his time, displays deductive gaps even at the very basic level[133] and is thus not complete – many things are simply presupposed but not stated, such as the fact that two lines do not enclose an area;[134] and operations such as addition, subtraction, multiplication, and division of magnitudes are used without them, or the laws they follow, ever being characterised, let alone defined.[135] And they do not display full universality, which can be seen, for example, in the fact that we find parallel proofs of cases which seem easily universalisable.[136]

Keeping this restriction in mind, we may even think that ancient mathematics of the fifth and fourth centuries BCE is a far cry from contemporary axiomatised systems. It is, nevertheless, a central predecessor to such systems,[137] and it was the one 'exact' science that philosophers like Aristotle could look to for laying

---

[129] We may understand *Posterior Analytics* 94a28–34 as an attempt to reconstruct a tiny part of a mathematical proof syllogistically.

[130] See Jope (1972).

[131] For biology as model science for Aristotle in the sense of fitting the model of demonstrative knowledge of the *Posterior Analytics* very closely, but yet a project fully established only with Aristotle, see Section 2.1.

[132] By completeness I understand that every item possesses its place in the system, none is missing, and all parts are clearly connected.

[133] See, for example, the different understandings of equality and congruence we find in *Elements* I, 4; see de Risi (2021), p. 315.

[134] See Heath (1956), vol. I, p. 232 and Proclus (1992), 196, 21.

[135] But there have been attempts to do a full axiomatization of Euclid I–IV in the twentieth century by Tarski and Mumia.

[136] See Mueller (1974), who on p. 43 names as examples VIII, 11 and 12; VI, 9 and 15; III, 5 and 6.

[137] According to Netz (1999), a small and well-formulated language makes inspection of the entire universe of mathematics possible, and in this way ancient mathematics may be closer to the closed set of rules modern proof theory employs than is usually given credit to anything going on before Frege.

down rules for exact sciences.[138] Given that mathematical propositions rely only on definitions, postulates, and common notions and the theorems established beforehand, ancient mathematics displays a degree of internal connectedness[139] that is much harder to achieve in philosophy. While the discussion of mathematics in philosophical texts shows that mathematics is frequently taken as a paradigmatic science, it is the points of universality and completeness that philosophers ultimately either raise as concerns or attempt to improve on in their philosophy.

As for completeness, we find that Plato in his *Republic* suggests that, in contrast to dialectics, mathematics cannot give a foundation to its axioms and thus is incomplete in this sense (see Section 2.2). And for Aristotle it is his own logical system that is complete in the sense of accounting for all valid inferences and forms a closed system (see *Prior Analytics* I, 23); he seems to have used mathematics as a model for deductive systems so far, but attempted to improve it in this respect.

While the importance of universality is stressed for deductions by Aristotle with the help of a geometrical example, as we can see in *Prior Analytics* I, 24, 41b13–22, it seems to be put in doubt by the role of geometrical constructions, and that means necessarily imperfect drawings and diagrams, for mathematical proofs. The fact that ancient mathematical deductions work with the help of constructions is essential for mathematical proofs at the time we are investigating in Greece. They cannot immediately be used by other axiomatised sciences and philosophy.[140] For example, *Elements* I, 4 starts the deduction with 'Let there be two triangles, ABC, DEF, having the two sides, AB, AC, equal to the two sides, DE, DF, respectively ... .' and either proceeds with a drawing or expects us to do a drawing in order to follow the proof.[141] Accordingly, the question presents itself what role these constructions play exactly.

3.1.2 The Role of Diagrams, Drawings, and Constructions

In proposition I, 32, usually a diagram of a triangle of the kind shown above is used for the proof. And constructions are in general used in Euclid's propositions.[142] This has given rise to two questions for philosophers: first, do

---

[138] And Euclid was seen as a paradigm for rigorous mathematical reasoning until the nineteenth century; see Mueller (1969), p. 289.

[139] In the sense that there is an immediate and clear connection between all parts, which is one aspect of completeness.

[140] Other sciences that also use drawings in an essential way, such as anatomy, are later disciplines, not yet around at the time we are focusing on (even if dissections were presumably made earlier in ancient Greece; see Aristotle *Posterior Analytics* 98a2).

[141] There are not many diagrams transmitted to us in manuscripts but a couple; see Netz (1999).

[142] This holds true of all the 'geometrical' books; in Book V, in which Euclid deals in general with proportions, and in his arithmetic Books, VII–IX, numbers and proportions are depicted with the help of lines.

the proofs in fact rely on these constructions and what would the consequences of such a dependence be; and second, do these constructions also give us existence proofs? Let us start with the first question.

Among modern historians of mathematics there is no consensus whether ancient mathematical proofs depended for their intelligibility on diagrams. For Netz, text and diagram cannot be taken apart as they make no sense without each other.[143] By contrast, Acerbi has argued that the diagram can always be reconstructed from the proposition. And Mendell has pointed out that while Acerbi's claim is logically true if the theorem is true and it is a good proof, we also find false diagrams in manuscripts and people failing to reconstruct an appropriate diagram.[144]

The first ancient thinker to raise a potential problem with the mathematical practise of drawing diagrams for their proofs seems to have been Protagoras. According to a passage in Aristotle's *Metaphysics* B, 997b35–998a4, Protagoras objected to the geometers that the circle touches the ruler not in a point, as the geometer assumes. Aristotle's report does not extend any further, but presumably, Protagoras' claim was that a circle drawn in the sand or on a wax tablet or on papyrus will touch a line in more than one point. In any case, Protagoras seems to have tried to refute the geometers by pointing out that their geometrical propositions do not hold of the drawings they in fact draw and that they are thus speaking falsely.

In addition to the problem that the drawings possess features that differ from those required for the proof in an essential way and thus are 'false' features, there are two further problems that the reliance of Greek mathematics on constructions for their proofs can raise for philosophers interested in deductions: First, while deductions are meant to be purely logical, independent of the perceptible world, mathematical proofs seem to rely in fact on something perceptible, the drawings. Secondly, while deductions are meant to give general conclusions, the usage of constructions seems to make them rely on individuals – this triangle drawn here – rather than on universals.[145] How do ancient mathematicians derive a merely logical structure producing universal results, if they start from individual examples? How can truth be preserved if we prove via individual instances that are full of imperfectness and seemingly depend on something we construct?

All three potential problems – drawings possess false features, are sensible, and are individual – are part of the background of Plato's discussion of the language of mathematics in his *Republic*. There Plato seems to criticise mathematicians for

---

[143] See especially Netz (1999), pp. 12 and 26.

[144] Acerbi (2020); Mendell in oral communication.

[145] Netz (1999) suggests that generality was achieved through extendability and repeatability of the proof.

philosophers took in questions and problems raised by mathematicians, it seems, however, much more likely that there was indeed some intellectual exchange between mathematicians and philosophers.

We may think that the method is prepared in the indirect proofs we find in Parmenides' poem, fragment 8 and that his indirect proofs were an inspiration for the form in which the incommensurability proofs were put. But Parmenides's proofs only show that F does not fit with what has been established before by Parmenides; they do not show as such that not-F has to hold independently of previous assumptions. This is something we only find with Zeno's paradoxes and the mathematical reductio ad absurdum proofs. Let us have a brief look at these.

Our best evidence for the incommensurability proof is preserved as an appendix to Euclid, Book X, Heiberg proposition 117. This version is an insertion into Euclid's text and shows some later reworking. But the core of the proof is a good deal older, going back to the Pythagoreans, sometime in the fifth century BCE. One version is mentioned by Aristotle, and according to Knorr there were half a dozen versions of the incommensurability proofs around.

The basic idea of this proof is the following: if we assume of a square *ABCD* the side *AB* and its diagonal *AC* to be commensurable, then we have to assume that the same number is both odd and even. This is a contradiction; thus they are incommensurable.

The main steps are as follows: we assume that *AC* and *AB* are commensurable with each other, hence they have a ratio equalling two numbers to each other; called *EF* and *g* (see Figure 6).[164] The version in Euclid also claims that 'these numbers be the least numbers in this ratio', but all that is in fact required is that they are not both even. It is then concluded that *EF* cannot be 'a unit', that is, 1, but has to be a number. 'For if *EF* is a unit, and has the ratio to *g* that *AC* has to *AB*, and *AC* is greater than *AB*, then *EF* is greater than the number *g*,[165] which is impossible.'[166]

---

[164] Using two letters for the first number and one for the second number is taken over from the original Greek text. Presumably two letters are used in the first case since in the course of the proof it is then assumed that the magnitude which this number represents is divided in half.

[165] Number being everything which is greater than 1.

[166] For the Pythagoreans, one as a unit is not a number and is both odd and even. Accordingly, showing that *EF* is not 1 is meant to exclude the possibility that we are dealing with something that for the Pythagoreans is odd and even, namely the 1. However, since *EF* is bigger than *g*, what would have been needed is a proof that *g* cannot be a unit; thus, this is one of the places where, according to Knorr, the reworked proof takes up an old Pythagorean proof without fully understanding it.

Given that the notion of the incommensurability of the side and diagonal would in fact never come up when measuring an empirical square in that such a measurement will always produce some result,[159] this proof shows that by the time it was discovered, Greek mathematics had clearly developed as a theoretical science independent of its practical applicability. The claim that such quantities are irrational is introduced through the very question posed and based solely on logical deduction.[160] The fact that incommensurability cannot be detected by the senses, may also have made it a discovery of special interest for Plato, who, as we have seen in Section 2, is very concerned about ways in which to lead students in their inquiries from the perceptible to the merely intelligible. Thus, it may not be a big surprise that Plato's texts are the first ones where we find the discovery of the incommensurable talked about.

Incommensurability is first mentioned in Plato's *Theaetetus*, but the imagined conversation between the young mathematician Theaetetus and Socrates does not refer to the square root of the number two, but to that of three and so forth up to seventeen (147dff.); hence, we are dealing with an already advanced stage of this discovery (the imagined date of the conversation is 399 BCE, the year of Socrates' trial and death). The discovery of the incommensurable has been suggested to be no later than the last quarter of the fifth century,[161] but this still leaves a lot of flexibility about the discovery in the fifth century. Given these problems of dating it is also hard to say whether the method of reductio was first developed by mathematicians and then taken up by philosophers or the route of influence was the other way round. Accordingly, there has been some debate in the scholarship about the relationship between the incommensurability proof and Eleatic method. Szabo has claimed that the mathematicians in fact could take up the logic of the method from the Eleatics.[162] Knorr, on the other hand, assumes that this is an old proof of the Pythagoreans,[163] which would allow for Zeno's paradoxical method to have been influenced through exposure to some version of the incommensurability proof. There is, of course, also the possibility that both the Pythagoreans and Zeno arrived at a similar method independently of each other at around the same time. Given that the Pythagoreans were involved in both what we would call mathematical and philosophical investigations simultaneously, and we have seen so far in several places the keen interest

---

Greek word *graphô* can mean either to draw or to prove, presumably coming from geometry proving by drawings.

[159] See Mueller (1980), p. 115.   [160] See Knorr (1975), pp. 2–4.   [161] See von Fritz (1970).
[162] Szabo (2004), pp. 148–149.
[163] A clear sign for the antiquity of the proof, according to Knorr (1975), is the usage of the dichotomy of odd and even and Aristotle's reference to it, as well as a step showing that one term is not a unit – an unnecessary step if the unit is considered to be an odd number, but necessary if, with Philolaus and Archytas, we assume the unit to be both odd and even.

using language that makes mathematics sound like a practical art; they use a language full of action words and give the impression as if geometrical objects came into being through the process of geometrical construction. In order to deal with these problems, Plato distinguishes what the language of the mathematicians expresses from what mathematics is really about.[146] And for Plato what mathematics is really concerned with is knowledge, which is immutable and stable and thus cannot depend on constructions. While the geometers talk as if the objects of their investigations were the visible drawings, this is only a *façon de parler*; their real objects are things like 'the square itself' or 'the diagonal itself' (510d–e); the constructions are just used as images. Accordingly, it seems that while Plato may be critical about the language used by the mathematicians in practise, he is not worried by Protagoras' claim that drawings possess false properties, and the perceptible and individual nature of constructions is unimportant given that, if correctly understood, they are simply tools the mathematicians use in order to grasp their real objects. Diagrams in geometry are only illustrations and do not belong to the essence of geometry.[147]

Similarly, Aristotle's answer to the problem raised is that geometers do not in fact rely on individuals: in *Posterior Analytics* 76b41–77a2 he reports the opinion that 'the geometer speaks falsely when he says that a line which is not a foot long is a foot long or a drawn line which is not straight is straight.' Against this opinion, Aristotle points out that 'the geometer does not conclude anything from the fact that the line which he himself has described is thus and so; rather, he relies on what this line shows.' So Aristotle clarifies that while geometers use individual and perceptible lines in their proofs, they do not conclude anything on the basis that this line is (or is indeed not) a foot long. Thus, it does not matter whether the line used is indeed a foot long.[148] The mathematicians just use it as an example to show whatever they want to demonstrate.[149] Defending geometers against Protagoras, Aristotle tries to make it clear that when geometers say something like 'let AB be a foot long', they are not referring to the concrete line that they draw in the sand.

We saw that the ancient philosophers who discuss the role of diagrams in ancient geometry take it for granted that geometers use constructions as a

---

[146] *Republic* Books VI and VII; especially 527a–b; see also Burnyeat (2000), pp. 39–41.

[147] Though construction as instruction which, e.g. determines the auxiliary figures involved in a proof, does belong to its essence.

[148] Accordingly, we may think of the geometers' practice as a predecessor for heuristic methods in philosophy.

[149] Thus, we may wonder whether the role of diagrams in ancient mathematics is analogous to the role of examples in philosophy. With Manders (2008) we could say that geometers rely only on 'co-exact properties' of geometric diagrams (i.e. on 'those conditions which are unaffected by some range of every continuous variation of a specified diagram') for their proofs, but not on 'exact conditions' (i.e. those which change once the diagram is subject to the smallest variation), as we see it in Euclid.

central part of their investigation, they are not debating whether diagrams play an integral role for mathematical proofs. The consequences they draw from this fact differ, however: while Protagoras assumes this to lead into serious problems for geometers, both Plato and Aristotle with their widely differing ontology try to show that in spite of the usage of perceptible, individual diagrams whose features do not match those of the things proven in important respects, mathematical proofs do not rely on something perceptible and individual. What they prove is ultimately not dependent on the object drawn. The diagrams are only representations of the real object of proof and so Plato and Aristotle are not worried that these representations do have features different from what is represented.

We should note that we do not seem to find a distinction in Plato's and Aristotle's discussion of mathematics between drawings that may be mere illustrations and constructions, on which Greek geometrical proofs arguably depend and which play a deductive role in proofs. One reason for this lack may be that understanding mathematics in principle as an ideal science in the way Plato and Aristotle do (of which mathematics in practise may fall short) does not allow for such a place for constructions.

Let us now move on to the second question mentioned earlier, whether these drawings also work as existence proofs. There is certainly mathematical language that suggests as much: Many propositions in Euclid contain a part that sounds like an existence claim: 'let there be' or 'let X be Y' (*estô*). For example, in proposition I, 4 we have 'Let ABC and DEF be two triangles ... '. Some scholars, prominently Zeuthen (1896), took the postulates to be existence assertions. Now the *estô* we get in Euclid is only an existence assumption (or, perhaps, an existence injunction, since it is an imperative); but not in itself a proof. But the construction that usually follows may be read as proving that some postulated mathematical object does indeed exist (for example, a triangle that possesses certain features).

Against such a reading, it has been objected[150] that we sometimes find several solutions to the same problem; for example, to the doubling of a cube or to the trisecting of an angle. This objection is not decisive, however, since nothing excludes the possibility that we can find different ways to prove one and the same existence. However, we do indeed not find any discussion of existence in Euclid's *Elements*, let alone something that is explicitly put forward as an existence proof. Euclid's justifications often do not show so much that an assertion is true, but that a performed operation is licensed. And Harari (2003) has claimed that understanding geometrical constructions as justifying

---

[150] E.g. by Knorr (1975).

the validity of a concept by presenting a particular instance that accords with it is a projection of the modern distinction in mathematics between definitions and existence that arose as a response to the discovery of paradoxical sets.

Nevertheless, the assertions of postulates in connection with the diagrams seems to have made philosophers think about existence proofs, at least in the context of criteria for the presentation of scientific reasoning and results. Accordingly, Aristotle is reading some of the mathematical problems we know from Euclid as existence proofs. For Aristotle, existence proofs are an important part of scientific inquiry – a science has to show for its basic kinds that they exist and what they are.[151] For Aristotle, these proofs do, however, not concern individuals, but universals;[152] and Aristotle is also clear that there can be no existence proofs for the basic principles. By contrast, Plato in his description of the mathematicians in the *Republic* criticises the mathematicians for taking their starting points as given without any further proof or justification, as we saw in Section 2.2.

3.2 Reductio ad Absurdum Proofs and Philosophical Paradoxes

Of the different mathematical methods of interest for philosophers, we will look at only one in a bit more detail, namely the method of reductio ad absurdum. The Latin term 'reductio ad absurdum' is a translation of the Greek expression *hê eis to adunaton apagôgê* (reductio to the impossible), which we find first in Aristotle's *Prior Analytics* 29b9. But Aristotle does not suggest that he is introducing this terminology for the first time.

In the kind of reductio proofs we will look at, the necessity of some p is proven by showing non-p to be impossible; accordingly, they require *tertium non datur* to hold.[153] These kinds of reductio proofs are of special interest, since they are a powerful method that we find both in mathematics and in philosophy for cases where we cannot find a direct proof.[154] They are central for the philosophical genre of paradoxes; most of Zeno's paradoxes work with such a reductio structure, for example. And there are lots of reductio proofs in Euclid.[155] Within a mathematical context, it seems likely that reductios were first developed for the proof of the development of the incommensurability of the side and the diagonal of the square – at least, this is a rather old Pythagorean

---

[151] See Section 4.1.   [152] See Harari (2003).   [153] Which Intuitionists doubt.
[154] Aristotle seems to assume in 62b38–40 that whatever can be proved indirectly can also be proved directly; but his own proof (in a wide sense) for the fundamentality of the principle of non-contradiction in his *Metaphysics* and the fact that he never mentions a direct proof for the incommensurability of the diagonal suggests that this may not hold of all indirect proofs.
[155] See, for example, *Elements* I, 6, 19, or 26; for an overview of the structure of Zeno's paradoxes, see Sattler (2021).

proof, and if Aristotle wants to give an example for a reductio, he usually refers to the incommensurability of the diagonal and the side of the square.[156] We will look at it as one relevant and important example that also raises interesting questions about the interaction between philosophers and mathematicians.

The incommensurability of the side and the diagonal was a special discovery in the development of Greek mathematics – a fact that is better understandable if we remind ourselves of its Pythagorean background. We saw in Section 1.1 that on a Pythagorean view, the world is set up as mathematically structured, according to (natural) numbers and relations that constitute them. Everything can be brought into a numerical relation to everything else. The discovery of the incommensurability shakes such a world view, for it shows that there are entities that cannot possibly be captured in terms of numerical ratios – the side and the diagonal of a square can never be brought into such a numerical relationship. So there are some things that seem to have no ratio, no *logos*; they are 'irrational'. And this seems to put the very idea of a rational cosmos into doubt.[157] Plato expresses the puzzlement about this finding in his *Laws*, 819c–820d, in a passage claiming that the Greeks assume we can measure all lengths and breadths against each other; thus most people are not aware that this is not possible for certain lengths and breadths.

Its effect on the mathematical community has seen different assessments by modern scholarship: Tannery (1887) thinks it led to a foundational crisis of mathematics not unlike the foundational crisis in mathematics at the end of the nineteenth century. By contrast, Knorr (1975), pp. 308 ff., takes it to be the background to the geometric style of number theory in Euclid's *Elements*, Book VII and the development of greater rigor in proportion theory; but he does not see it as a crisis in Greek mathematics. However, also Knorr thinks that the problem of the incommensurability engaged the effort of the most notable mathematicians of the fourth century, Theodorus, Theatetus, Archytas, and Eudoxus. It was a crucial force motivating Eudoxus's theory of proportion which is the foundation of Euclid's proportion theory in *Elements*, Book V. And it seems to have been one important factor for the increasing dominance of geometrical proofs – it shows that there are some things in mathematics, like the relation of the diagonal of a square to its sides, that cannot be dealt with arithmetically, but only geometrically.[158]

---

[156] See, for example, 41a26–27 or 430a31; and see also Knorr (1975). In *Prior Analytics* II, 11 Aristotle shows how reductio ad absurdum works in general. Szabó (2004), however, claims *Elements* IX, 30 (an odd number, if it measures an even number, must also measure its half) to be the oldest indirect proof.

[157] This strong effect on the Pythagorean world view explains why we are told that the person discovering the incommensurability was allegedly drowned by his Pythagorean community – whether or not this story is in fact true.

[158] See also Plato's depiction of a math lesson in his *Theaetetus* where we hear from young Theaetetus that his teacher Theodorus was 'demonstrating with the aid of diagrams' – the

Philosophy of Mathematics from the Pythagoreans to Euclid 51

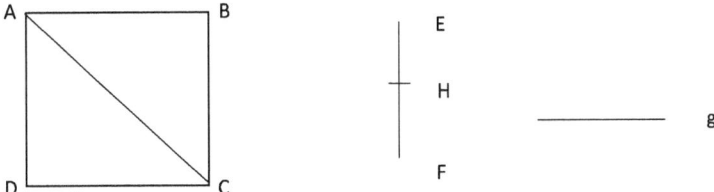

Figure 6 Proof for the incommensurability of the diagonal and the side of a square.

In a second step it is shown that *EF* has to be even, since it has the same ratio to *g* as *AC* has to *AB*, and the square of *AC* is double that of *AB*; if it is double something, it has to be even:

EF:*g* = *AC*:*AB*,

$(AC)^2 = 2 \times (AB)^2$

=> *EF* is even.

In a third step, it is demonstrated that *g* has to be odd, for otherwise *EF* and *g* would both be even and could not be relatively prime. In a fourth and final step, it is assumed that *EF* is divided in half by *H*, which shows that *g* has to be even. For the square of *EF* has to be four times the square of *EH* (*EF* being double *EH*), but also double of that of *g*, which in turn means that the square of *g* is double that of *EH*. Accordingly, 'the square of *g* is even, and thus *g* is even' (if it were odd, its square would be odd).

$EF = 2 \times EH$;

$(EF)^2 = 4 \times (EH)^2$;

$(EF)^2 = 2 \times g^2$

=> $g^2 = 2 \times (EH)^2$

=> *g* is even.

But in the third step it was shown that *g* is odd, so *g* has to be both odd and even, which is impossible. Thus the assumption of *AC* and *AB* being commensurable leads to a contradiction.

We find the main idea of the way in which this proof works also in many paradoxes of Zeno: in order to show that motion, plurality, or *topos* (place/space) are problematic, it is first assumed that there is a plurality, motion, or *topos* before it is shown that this very assumption leads to inconsistencies.

Like in the incommensurability proof, so also in Zeno's paradoxes, what is used as a starting point is the opposite of what is shown to be the result in the end. In the incommensurability proof we start with the assumption that *AB* and *AC* are commensurable, while Zeno uses as a starting point one that is not his own, but widely held, the position of a pluralist. And from this starting point it is then shown that plurality, motion, and *topoi* are problematic in themselves.

Both Zeno and mathematical reductio proofs start from a position they do not share and then show that this position leads to contradictions – that the same number has to be odd and even, that the same distance has to be finite and infinite, and so on. And this contradiction shows that the position implying it is false absolutely. In comparison to Parmenides's indirect proofs, such reductios can be seen to be much stronger because

(a) they make sure we do not introduce our own assumptions which the opponent may not share; and
(b) the opponent is refuting herself – in the very act of thinking she is undermining herself.

For the realm of mathematics, it is a good and strong proof, as it is for Zeno who is the founder of the genre of paradoxes.[167] The reason these proofs work very well here is that they work within a framework in which it is clear that I have only two alternatives – either *AB* and *AC* are commensurable or they are incommensurable, either we can consistently think of a plurality of things or we cannot.

For later philosophers starting with Aristotle, however, this method of proof ultimately needed further refinement, since in many philosophical contexts showing that F cannot hold does not in itself demonstrate that not-F holds. Accordingly, it is not necessarily seen as a strong proof and can only be used in certain contexts.

For the mathematicians, the particular usage of this method to prove the incommensurability of the side and the diagonal of the square seems to have been one reason that led to a sharper distinction between arithmetic and geometry, to a geometric style of number theory, and to shifting the burden of proofs to geometry.

4 Central Concepts of Philosophy and Mathematics

This section will investigate important concepts that were originally developed either within a mathematical setting and then became central for

---

[167] See Sattler (2021).

philosophy, or in a discussion to which philosophers and mathematicians both seem to have contributed. It starts with a discussion of the notion of a principle or starting point of an argument or proposition in Aristotle and Euclid. We will then consider one central concept in natural philosophy that developed under the influence of mathematics, namely continuity, by looking at the oldest philosophical explanation of continuity in Parmenides's poem, at the reflection of mathematical treatments of continuity we find in the Pseudo-Aristotelian treatise *On Indivisible Lines*, and at passages of Euclid's *Elements*. This will show that the most important account of continuity in ancient Greek thought, the one developed by Aristotle in his *Physics*, rests on the mathematical treatment of geometrical objects as being always further divisible while also taking up Eleatic terminology. Closely linked to the understanding of continuity is the notion of limits and of infinity. For the latter, we will leave out the philosophical strand of the discussion in Anaximander, Anaxagoras, and Democritus and concentrate on the mathematically inspired strand of this debate that shows up in some of Zeno's paradoxes and may be assumed in the method of exhaustion in Book XII of Euclid's *Elements*. It is this mathematical understanding that Aristotle takes up, trying to show that it requires only a potential, not an actual infinity. There are in principle several other important concepts – like the notion of necessity or of proportion – that developed in some form of interplay between philosophy and mathematics but that we will not be able to look at here for reasons of space.

4.1 Principles and Starting Points

4.1.1 Principles in Euclid

Deducing from first principles (*archai*)[168] is specific for Greek mathematics and not to be found in Egyptian and Babylonian mathematics. We saw in the previous section that for an axiomatised science, according to Aristotle, two points are central: the rules of deduction, and the principles or axioms which serve as starting points for proofs. While we discussed rules of deduction in the previous section, we will deal with starting points here.

Such starting points themselves cannot be proven, but have to be taken as given. What exactly these principles are, has changed over time, as we can see in mathematics from the fact that the number of starting points in Euclid does not match the number in Hilbert, who assumes twenty axioms. If we look at the

---

[168] The Greek word *archê* carries with it connotations of truth, beginning, origin, and fundamentality, which I try to convey by the title of this section, 'principles and starting points'.

beginning of Euclid's *Elements*, we see that he bases mathematics on three kinds of first principles – definitions, postulates, and common notions:

1. Definitions of the basic concepts used

Many books of the *Elements* start with a set of definitions that are relevant for the respective book. Book I, for example, on plane rectilinear geometry, starts with the definitions of point, line, surface, and different plane angles; while the arithmetical Book VII starts with the definitions of unit and number.

In addition to definitions, we find in Book I (and only there) two other kinds of principles:

2. Postulates

Euclid presents five different postulates that seem to be instructions for construction processes in geometry (such as to draw a straight line from any point to any point). At least this characterization holds true of the first three postulates. By contrast, the fourth postulate, claiming that 'all right-angles are equal to each other' does not refer to something to be done and has been interpreted as either equivalent to or presupposing a principle of invariability of figures or the homogeneity of space.[169] And the fifth postulate, the parallel-postulate, has come under heavy attack since antiquity – later mathematicians either attempted to prove it as a theorem or to replace it by some other definition of parallels. Like the first three postulates, it seems to ensure the existence of a geometrical object, in this case the meeting point of two lines (if they are not parallels). But it also implicitly presupposes that we are dealing with the geometry of flat, not curved, spaces, and accordingly does not hold for what since the nineteenth century has been developed as non-Euclidean geometry.

3. Common notions

While the postulates in Euclid are specific for geometry, the common notions are, as their name suggests, common to more than one science; in the context of Euclid's *Elements*, they apply to geometry and arithmetic equally. Modern editions usually print five common notions (for example, the first common notion reads 'Things equal to the same thing are also equal to one another'); but additional ones have been added later on, and there is also a dispute whether these five were originally in Euclid.[170] Since the third one ('if equals are

---

[169] See Heath (1956), p. 200.
[170] Tannery (1884), p. 221 claims that they were not originally in Euclid, but added later on, since they are oddly positioned – we have postulates peculiar for geometry before the notions common to different mathematical sciences. By contrast, Heath (1956) thinks that the position of the common notions is rather natural. It would have been even more awkward to separate the postulates from the definitions by putting the postulates after the common notions, since the postulates prove the existence of some of what is defined. And since Aristotle speaks about common notions in the plural, Heath thinks it is likely that at least the first three common

Philosophy of Mathematics from the Pythagoreans to Euclid 55

subtracted from equals, the remainders are equal') is frequently given by Aristotle as an example of a common notion, it has the clearest claim to being an old common notion. But the fact that it is unclear how many common notions there were indeed in Euclid, how we should understand the genre of postulates, and the fact that we do not find any reflection in the *Elements* about how definitions, postulates, and common notions are connected show that the question what kinds of principles are necessary for the science of mathematics was not sufficiently clarified.

Especially the relationship between postulates and common notions has been a matter of debate. It has been proposed to understand postulates as domain specific, since they belong specifically to the domain of geometry, while common notions are universal as they pertain equally to geometry and arithmetic. As a distinction between the two, it has also been suggested that postulates can be confirmed by demonstration, while common notions are incapable of proof. Finally, the difference has also been framed as one between practical and theoretical: postulates seem to be practical, as they refer to something done or to be done, while common notions seem to be theoretical since they refer to something known. Understanding the difference like this seems to correspond to the distinction between problems and theorems that we find in Euclid's propositions.[171]

Theorems are what in modern terms would be called propositions, asserting that all figures of a certain class possess some characteristic (for example, 'In any triangle, the greater side subtends the greater angle', I, 18; 'quod erat demonstrandum'; using an all-quantifier), while problems call for constructing a figure with certain characteristics (for example, to construct a pentagon, IV, 11; 'quod facit demonstrandum'; using an existential-quantifier). The difference between theorems and propositions can also be captured as one between knowing that and knowing how.[172]

Especially the closeness of the last distinction between postulate and common notions to the one between propositions and theorem makes the lack of any explicit reflection on the status of and the relation between the different kinds of

---

notions of Euclid were taken over from earlier mathematicians. These are the ones that a lot of theorems in Euclid rely upon and that most modern interpreters take to be authentic. For a recent survey of the evidence for their authenticity, see de Risi (2021).

[171] See also Harari (2003), p. 2 who frames it as a 'correspondence between the two types of first principles and the two types of derived propositions'.

[172] The older geometers regarded a theorem as directed at proving what is proposed, a problem as directed at constructing what is proposed. See also Proclus 77, 7–81, 22. Harari (2003) understands the distinction between problems and theorems as 'a distinction between two types of proofs: proofs that establish the correctness of certain constructions and proofs that establish the truth of certain assertions'.

starting points in Euclid (and presumably also in specimens of the *Elements* genre written before Euclid) strongly felt. Accordingly, in order to understand the different types of starting points of the ancient mathematicians better, it is helpful to have a look at the most important discussion of different starting points for sciences before Euclid, namely at this discussion in Aristotle's *Posterior Analytics*.

4.1.2 Principles in Aristotle

It is in Aristotle's *Posterior Analytics* that we find the first systematic reflection on the question what a principle of a science amounts to and which different kinds of principles there are. While Aristotle makes it clear that he takes over the term 'axiom' from the mathematicians (*Metaphysics* 1005a20), it is in his *Analytics* that a first systematic account of different kinds of principles is developed[173] and that we find a first explicit discussion of how axioms have to be characterised in order to work as first principles of a science.[174] He characterises principles as follows:

> I call principles in each kind those things which it is not possible to prove that they are. *What* the first principles and what follows from these mean, is assumed. *That* they are is necessary to assume for the principles and demonstrated for the others. For example, what a unit is or what straight or a triangle are; that units and magnitudes are, this is assumed, but everything else is proven. (76a31–36)

Aristotle gives a systematic account of different kinds of principles for sciences in general, while the examples he uses derive from mathematics. For him, the examples used – unit, straight, and triangle – have three different statuses in the science of principles: a unit is a first principle where we have to assume what and that it is; 'straight' is a feature (*pathê*) of lines;[175] and 'triangle' is one of the things that follow from the first principles in geometry without itself being a first principle. In the latter two cases, *what* they are is assumed, while *that* they are has to be demonstrated.

Aristotle makes it clear that principles are that from which a proof starts, while they are in turn unprovable (otherwise we would either get into an infinite regress or a circular proof). He distinguishes *axioms* as general principles from *theses* which are specific to an individual science.[176] The axioms themselves

---

[173] This also includes coining an important part of the language for further discussion.
[174] See von Fritz (1955), pp. 33–35.   [175] See 76b15.
[176] In *Posterior Analytics* I, 2, however, he seems to distinguish between axiom and thesis by pointing out that axioms must be grasped by anyone wanting to learn anything, while theses need not be grasped by anyone. But these two characterisations fit together, since people not interested in science A but only science B need not be concerned with the theses of science A, while a grasp of axioms as common principles seems to be necessary for people interested in

Philosophy of Mathematics from the Pythagoreans to Euclid 57

divide into two groups: first, propositions that are true of everything, as, for example, the law of non-contradiction; they have to be known by everybody who wants to have any kind of scientific knowledge. The sciences do not reason from them, but rather in accordance with them. Second, there are propositions common to several sciences, for example, 'if equals are taken from equals, equals remain', which is relevant only for sciences dealing with quantities. This last example is one of the common notions we find in Euclid; while it is an example Aristotle takes over from the mathematicians, it is Aristotle who gives this kind of principle a systematic place.

Theses are divided into *definitions*, which say what something is, and *hypotheses*, which say that something is or is not. There is a debate whether the latter refers to existential propositions, that is, x exists, or to predicative statements, that is, x is y.[177] For the time being I follow the first interpretation, which suggests that while definitions are concerned with the essence of the scientific objects,[178] hypotheses are concerned with their existence.[179] The existence of the most basic objects of a science, like the point in geometry, usually has to be assumed, while the existence of more complex objects has to be proven, in geometry usually by construction.

What can be used as such premises, as starting points for our conclusions? Do these principles have to be necessary or can they be contingent? Do they even have to be true? We do not find any answers to these questions in Euclid. But we find outlines of a first philosophical discussion of such principles in Plato's example of the line in his *Republic*. Aristotle characterises such first principles or premises as follows in his *Posterior Analytics*:

> 'If, then, understanding is as we posited, it is necessary for demonstrative understanding in particular to depend on things which are true and primitive and immediate and more familiar than and prior to and explanatory of the conclusion' (71b20–25).

---

different sciences. We should also bear in mind that the terminology is not always fully stable in Aristotle and seems to have been in flux also in mathematics.

[177] For the first reading, see, for example, Barnes (1993), pp. 100–101, for the second, Harari (2003). For the second reading, we find support in passages like *Posterior Analytics* 92b4–8 which seems to suggest, according to Harari, that 'the possibility of answering the question "what it is" serves as a criterion for distinguishing existent objects from non-existent objects'. The first interpretation can rely on passages such as 92b19–25, which seems to make it explicit that a definition does not yet settle if what it accounts for is indeed possible.

[178] Without making any statements about existence, so a definition could concern Leibniz's regular polyhedron with ten faces, which cannot exist, but can be defined. (For a different view, claiming that for Aristotle 'the existence of an entity is determined by means of definitions', see Harari (2003)).

[179] In Aristotle's *Physics* we see that he usually expects a scientific treatise to deal with both, for example, the question what time is and whether it exists.

Thus we must proceed from starting points that are given six characterisations,[180] three of them absolute, and three relative. Given that we are dealing with premises for demonstrative sciences, our starting points have to be true, they have to be primitive in the sense that they are not derived from others, and immediate in the sense that they cannot be gained from a syllogism with a middle-term – these are the absolute characterisations. The relative ones tell us that these principles are more familiar than other things, in the sense that they are better known to us; they are prior to others in the sense that they have to be assumed in order to understand what builds on them, and finally they also have to be explanatory of the conclusions.

Given that these principles have nothing prior to them, they themselves cannot be proven, at least not in the same way as what is based on them can,[181] or not in the same science as for which they are principles.[182] Instead, they have to be what we would call self-evident; what Aristotle characterises as

> what must be and what must be thought because of itself. For there is no external proof (*logos*) for it nor demonstration (*apodeixis*), but only one in the soul; since there is no syllogism. For one can always block an external argument, but not always an internal one. (76b23–27)

So these basic principles (a) exist through themselves; and (b) we believe them through themselves; that is, they are not known through an inference, but rather through a kind of internal understanding that does not rely on anything else.

4.1.3 Comparison between Aristotle and Euclid

If we now compare Aristotle's and Euclid's understanding of principles, we see that they share important commonalities. For both, at least some principles are definitions, and definitions of the basic items are fundamental (we may even suggest that they share a common understanding of what definitions should do). These basic items cannot be proven while the existence of what builds on these has to be proven – Aristotle's claim that it has to be shown 'that they are' fits, at least to some degree, Euclid's postulates where existence may be understood to be proven by constructions. For both thinkers, definitions make it clear what so-and-so is, but assert nothing about the existence of the thing defined, as can be seen in Euclid, for example, when he defines a square in definition I, 22 but does

---

[180] The exact understanding of these six characterisations has seen different interpretations; see von Fritz (1955), pp. 21–24 and McKirahan (1992), pp. 24ff.

[181] Some may allow for indirect proofs of the kind Aristotle suggests for the principle of non-contradiction in his *Metaphysics* Γ, showing that everybody who denies this principle has already to embrace it in order to be able to formulate any denial.

[182] Plato's *Republic* may be read as suggesting that dialectic can also prove principles for other disciplines.

not assume its existence until after I, 46, when it has been constructed,[183] and is explicated by Aristotle in his *Posterior Analytics* II.[184]

Furthermore, both Aristotle and Euclid work with common notions, even if the language they use for labelling these principles that are common to several sciences is not exactly the same.[185] Aristotle claims that the mathematicians restrict such common notions as 'equals taken from equals leave equals' to their respective field, while in principle it holds for all quantitative things and is as such investigated in the area of what he calls first philosophy, that is, metaphysics (*Metaphysics* XI, 4, 1061b17–27).

Aristotle and Euclid differ, however, in some of the concrete definitions they give; for example, the point is defined by Euclid as 'that which has no parts', while for Aristotle this is not enough; we also need to add that it has a position, in order to distinguish it from the unit. Here we may follow Proclus' assumption that a point is the only partless thing that is a subject matter of geometry, so that the further qualification we find in Aristotle's account can be left out in Euclid, given the context. But a definition like Euclid's of a straight line as 'that which lies evenly with the points on itself' would, according to Heath, be an unscientific definition for Aristotle, since 'lies evenly' can only be understood with the help of the notion of a straight line, which is what is meant to be defined.[186] And, in contrast to Euclid, Aristotle has a fully fledged theory of definitions.

Investigating what the role of a definition is and what can count as an appropriate definition starts in philosophy with Socrates and is developed by Plato in important ways. Aristotle makes it clear that a definition of X must be essentially predicated of X and only of X (while the individual attributes in a definition taken separately will apply more widely). And a definition that is not of first principles must be expressed in terms of things prior to what is to be defined. (This criterion is what Euclid's definition of a line also seems to violate.)

We find three different kinds of definition in Aristotle: first, indemonstrable definitions of primary terms; second, real or causal definitions in which the content of a syllogism is packed into a single proposition; and third, nominal definitions. Aristotle discusses causal and nominal definitions when examining the question whether definitions can be proven (*Posterior Analytics* II, 7–10), showing that they appear in a demonstration either as a premise or are in a way identical to the whole demonstration.

---

[183] But see Harari (2003) for a different understanding.
[184] Existence questions in arithmetic could be questions like whether a certain number (e.g., a prime between 20 and 30) does indeed exist.
[185] See Heath (1956), p. 120. The label 'common notions' may in fact not be by Euclid; see de Risi (2021), p. 302.
[186] Plato, *Parmenides* 137e claims 'straight' to be whatever has its middle in front of both its ends, which is also quoted by Aristotle.

Furthermore, Aristotle also deals with principles that are important for *all* scientific knowledge, such as the principle of non-contradiction, while we do not find any axioms of that kind of generality in Euclid. On the other hand, the practical aspect of some of Euclid's postulates that lies in the constructions required would not fit Aristotle's theory of science.

Overall, however, we seem to find a principal alignment between the two: Aristotle's common axioms correspond to Euclid's common notions, his definitions (*horismoi*) more or less to Euclid's definitions (*horoi*); and his hypotheses are akin to Euclid's postulates (insofar as they can be understood as assertions of existence).[187]

Euclid's specific distinction between definitions, postulates, and common notions does not suggest he has read Aristotle very much. But it has been suggested that both may draw from a common source.[188]

The genre of 'Elements', to which Euclid's work belongs, does in itself declare that it is dealing with basic mathematical principles or starting points – it is not attempting to present new research, but rather to put the current mathematical knowledge in a 'systematic' form. According to Eudemus, there were at least three earlier *Elements* around before Euclid: the first by Hippocrates of Chios, one by Leon, and one by Theudius of Magnesia; the last one was written in the surrounding of Plato's Academy.[189] Accordingly, at least some *Elements* came into being in the vicinity of flourishing philosophical debates.[190] This may explain why Philodemus called Plato the architect of mathematics. Aristotle in his *Analytics* probably refers to the third generation of *Elements*, to Theudius.[191]

Let us now move on to other notions of importance for both mathematicians and philosophers.

4.2 Mathematical and Philosophical Notions of Continuity

The most important conception of continuity[192] in ancient times is Aristotle's account.[193] It is developed as an account for physical magnitudes, but yet it

---

[187] Though three of Euclid's postulates license construction and we find nothing equivalent to this in Aristotle.

[188] And Harari (2003) claims that 'Euclid's introduction of the distinction between definitions and postulates seems to correspond to Aristotle's distinction between definitions and existence claims. That is to say, the introduction of three types of first principles seems to stem from the attempt to accommodate the structure of the *Elements* with Aristotle's requirement, according to which the existence of the defined terms should be established.'

[189] See Proclus (1992) 66.4–67.12.

[190] We do not know whether these early *Elements* contained only propositions or also definitions, common notions, and postulates. It may be that the philosophical discussions about starting points in Plato's Academy (which, of course, included the young Aristotle) led to them being eventually included in the genre of *Elements*.

[191] See Heath (1921), p. 321.

[192] For more details concerning this section, see Sattler (2020b).

[193] For a modern take on Aristotle's understanding of continuity, see Hellman and Shapiro (2018).

explicitly takes up mathematical insights. By understanding continua as what is always further divisible into divisibles without ever getting to zero extension or indivisible atoms, Aristotle's account of continuity is the philosophical alternative to atomism.

The first philosophical account of continuity in the history of thought can already be found in Parmenides in the fifth century BCE. For him, something is continuous if it is homogenous in every respect, which means displaying no differences of kind, quality, or quantity.[194] As a result of this uninterrupted homogeneity, continua are indivisible according to Parmenides: divisions are only possible where there are differences; since there are no internal differences in a continuum, it is completely indivisible.

Drawing the inference from complete homogeneity to indivisibility is supported by some paradoxes of Zeno, Parmenides' student, which demonstrate the problems we get into if we assume continua like magnitudes and motion to be divisible. For example, in one of his motion paradoxes, called the 'dichotomy' or 'runner paradox' (fragment DK29A25), Zeno raises the problem of how to conceptualize a finite motion, like that of a runner covering a finite race course AB in a finite time FG. To do so, she first has to cover half of the course AC, and then again the first half of the remaining half CD, then DE, ad infinitum (see Figure 7).

Thus it seems a runner has to cover an infinite number of spatial parts in order to cover a finite distance in a finite time. For a spatial distance seems to contain infinitely many parts, all of which have to be covered. Given that we cannot pass infinitely many spatial parts in a finite time, the paradox seems to suggest that motion cannot be conceptualized.[195]

In one of his plurality paradoxes,[196] Zeno shows that if we take some physical magnitude to be divisible at one point (without this point being legitimised by any internal differences), then the magnitude is divisible everywhere; but if divisible everywhere, it can also be divided everywhere,[197] and we never reach consistent parts in this way. For either these parts have no extension, so that we

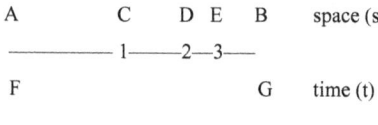

Figure 7 Zeno's runner paradox.

---

[194] See Sattler (2019).
[195] For a detailed discussion of the motion paradoxes, see Sattler (2020a), chapter 3.
[196] Simplicius (2011), *In Phys.* 139.19-140.6, Lee (1967), fragments 1 and 2.
[197] This step from being divisible to being divided and thus from possibility to actuality is objected to by Aristotle.

face the problem of how some extended physical whole can be composed of extensionless parts. Or these parts have some extension, in which case either this shows we are not yet done with our division and our parts are indeterminate; or the parts seem to be infinitely many,[198] in which case they seem to lead to an infinite extension. Zeno raises these and similar paradoxes for physical continua. Mathematical replies to them have often been suggested, based on modern mathematical developments such as the possibility of calculating the sum of an infinite convergent series, mathematical functions since Cauchy, and the limit of a function. But it remains a question whether a solely mathematical reply is sufficient for the problems they raise for the physical realm.[199]

Mathematical atomism of the kind we find in the pseudo-Aristotelian treatise *On Indivisible Lines*[200] seems to have responded to these paradoxes, as we can see from the fact that the need to avoid Zeno's paradoxes is mentioned as one of the points in favour of the assumption of indivisible lines. The basic idea of atomism here is that we can only divide magnitudes up to a certain point, before we hit indivisibles. The parts derived by division thus will never be infinite.

Also Aristotle's account of continuity is meant to show, among other things, how a physical theory of continuity can reply to these Zenonian paradoxes. Aristotle gives us two different characterisations of continuity:

(1) Continuous are those things whose limit, at which they touch, is one (*Physics* V, 3).
(2) Continuous is that which is divisible into what is always further (or infinitely) divisible (*Physics* VI, 2).

The first account of continuity is two-place, 'A is continuous with B', while the second is one-place, 'A is continuous'. Aristotle does not explain why he gives us two different accounts, but he moves freely between the two, which thus seem to be closely related.

Understanding extended magnitudes as being divisible without end is one of the crucial notions Aristotle employs from a mathematical context in order to set up a science of locomotion in his *Physics*. At first glance, the suggestion that Aristotle takes up a mathematical understanding may not seem very plausible.

---

[198] Zeno does not explain in this paradox why they are infinitely many. They may seem to be infinitely many since from a certain point onwards such divisions will be beyond what is perceptible, or, because between any two parts there has to be a further one in between to guarantee that they are indeed different parts, as he claims in DK29B3.
[199] For details, see Sattler (2020a), chapter 3.
[200] Geometrical atomism of the kind reflected in this treatise was defended by Xenocrates in Plato's Academy. In Plato's *Timaeus* we saw a form of atomism that assumes smallest triangles as atomistic building blocks, and in Aristotle's *Physics*, Book VI we find arguments against point atomism.

Philosophy of Mathematics from the Pythagoreans to Euclid 63

For we do not find a discussion or explicit definition of '*suneches*', the Greek term translated as 'continuous', in the mathematical texts handed down to us from the time up to Aristotle. And most of the occurrences of the term *suneches* in Euclid refer to a continued proportion.[201]

We have, however, clear indications that the mathematicians understood lines, surfaces, and solids as continua in the Aristotelian sense: there are a few passages in the *Elements* in which Euclid uses the term *suneches* as being successive in the way continuous lines are – so as continuous in a two-place sense (*AB* is continuous with *BC*).[202] And *On Indivisible Lines* makes it clear that a one-place understanding of continuity is presupposed by geometers, since they treat their geometrical objects as being always further divisible for their mathematical activities (969b20ff.). When they assume crossing lines and similar constructions, there is no reflection of atomistic worries, such as that a line crossing another would need to go between two atoms; rather, infinite divisibility is simply assumed.[203] And Aristotle himself in *Physics* III claims the mathematicians to understand magnitudes in this sense (203b17–18).

Aristotle's own work is central for establishing an account of continuity within natural philosophy and for contrasting it to what is discrete. His *Categories* (4b20) is the first text demonstrating that quantities can be divided into discrete and continuous ones. It gives an argument for understanding numbers as discrete and lines as continuous. The fact that Aristotle does not simply take it for granted in his *Categories* that numbers are discrete, but thinks he has to argue for there being no contact between the parts of numbers, shows that he is not taking over ready-made terminology. But Aristotle's primary examples for demonstrating what being discrete and being continuous mean are from the realm of mathematics – numbers and lines. So Aristotle seems to take up a distinction that is implicitly there in mathematical thinking. By employing and expanding Eleatic terminology – the term *suneches* plays a crucial role with the Eleatics but the notion of discretenessis is not to be found – Aristotle introduces the distinction between continuity and discreteness explicitly into the philosophical realm.

From the mathematicians Aristotle can take up a one-place as well as a two-place understanding of continuous quantities, on which his two different accounts of continuity are based. For him continua are homogenous, but in contrast to Parmenides, they only need to be homogenous in the genus in question and can allow for differences in other respects. And in contrast to the Eleatic inference that what is continuous has to be indivisible, Aristotle agrees

---

[201] See, e.g., VIII, 8. [202] See Book XI, 1; Book I, postulate 2; and Book IV, 16.
[203] See also Proclus (1992), 277, 25.

with the mathematicians that continua are divisible wherever we want, ad infinitum.

But Aristotle is not simply transferring the mathematical understanding of magnitudes to physics. Rather he adopts it for the physical realm, as becomes clear when he discusses the difference between continuity and contiguity. While for mathematicians, two lines in the same plane that touch are continuous and one,[204] in physical contexts, two things that are continuous do not become one thing simply by touching. Accordingly, for Aristotle continuous things (a) possess touching limits (which suffices for continuity in mathematics) and (b) these limits have to be one, so that these objects move as one whole and are not only neighbouring things (an additional requirement for the physical realm) (*Physics* V, 3).

Aristotle's understanding of continuity is closely linked to his account of limits and of infinity: we will briefly look at these two in the following sections 4.3 and 4.4.

4.3 Limits – the Distinction between Inner and Outer Limits

What delimits one thing from another? This question has been raised as a problem for natural philosophy by Zeno, but Aristotle's answer is important also for the philosophy of ancient mathematics. Zeno claims in fragment DK29B3 that any plurality of things seems to be the very number it is; let us say there are two things, A and B. At the same time this plurality has to be infinitely many because between every two things there has to be another thing. For in order to ensure that A and B are indeed two separate things, there must be some other thing C in between. But then we also need a thing between A and C, and C and B to separate them from each other, ad infinitum.[205] Natural philosophers reacted to this paradox by pointing out that what separates one thing from another need not be another thing. For example, with the atomists it is the void that guarantees the separateness of two things, between two atoms as well as between two phenomenal things.

Also Aristotle does not assume that we need a further thing to separate two things, but only what he calls a limit: each physical magnitude possesses limits that are not themselves things nor extended parts. Limits possess one dimension less than what they limit; for example, the limits of a one-dimensional line are points and thus without extension. Limits that delimit a magnitude from its surrounding are external limits. For Aristotle, continua also have what we can call 'inner limits', i.e. division points that mark off possible parts *within* a continuum. Usually these division points are not given, but they can be

---

[204] As long as they do not simply intersect or form an angle.   [205] See Sattler (2020b).

constructed wherever we like. For example, if we measure a long plank with a small ruler, we mark off parts of the plank with the help of such marks. Outer limits separate one whole from another; they guarantee the unity of a continuum vis-à-vis other continua. Inner limits, by contrast, guarantee the internal unity of a continuum by showing that we can divide it wherever we please without ever finding a gap.

This distinction between inner and outer limits of continua is the first predecessor of the modern distinction between points lying anywhere within an interval and the end points of such an interval. Furthermore, the modern distinction between closed and open intervals, that is, between intervals which contain their end points and those that do not, can be seen as prefigured in Aristotle's analysis of the outer limits that are of most concern to him in his *Physics*, namely those between motion and rest. Aristotle makes it clear that if a moving thing slows down and comes to a standstill, there is no last point of motion nor a first point of rest; for every point within a motion we may choose, there will always be another one closer to the limit between motion and rest. Thus, he is the first to clarify that there is no first or last point *within* a continuous interval. The limit between motion and rest can be seen in analogy to the way we think of the limit of a continuous open interval nowadays: it is the point of an interval that in contrast to all other possible points does not have an ε-neighbourhood.[206]

We will not be able to discuss the notion of a limit further here. Instead, we will now move on to infinity.

4.4 Philosophical and Mathematical Notions of Infinity

With the notion of infinity (*apeiron*) we are dealing with a notion that from early on was important for mathematics as well as for physics – being about quantities in general, it is relevant for mathematics, but it also plays a role in discussions about the world as a whole and thus for physics. The mathematicians also deal with one-dimensional infinite extensions, of which we can have a plurality, such as the infinite lines we find in Euclid. By contrast, the natural philosophers discuss infinite extension with respect to bodies and thus as something three-dimensional, so that there could at most be one of these. For if more than one of these infinite bodies were to exist, these infinite bodies would limit each other and thus not be infinite any longer, as, for example, Gorgias argues.[207]

---

[206] Intuitively speaking, an ε-neighbourhood of a point is a set of points surrounding this point within a certain distance, called ε, such that one can move to and fro without leaving the set. Somewhat more formally, for a given point a on the real number line and some positive number ε, $\varepsilon > 0$, we call the ε-neighbourhood of a the set of all numbers x such that the distance between x and a is less than ε.

[207] See MXG 979b20–27 in Aristotle (1995) and Sextus, *Adv. Mathem.* VII, 69–70.

The philosophers seem to be aware of the mathematical usage there is of that notion and attempt to preserve it in their conception of infinity. But while the intensive philosophical discussion about infinity, which started at least with Zeno and finds a full reply in Aristotle, may make us expect to find a reflection of it with the mathematicians, there is none to be found in Euclid.

In philosophy, being *apeiron* is a central notion almost from the very beginning, starting with Anaximander. The Greek word *apeiron* is formed with the help of the alpha privative that is usually understood as added to the Greek word for limit or end, *peras*; so *apeiron* is that which is without limit or end; it is not quantifiable. There is no systematic distinction between what is infinite and what is unbounded with the ancient Greeks; and our modern distinction between countable ($\mathbb{N}$, $\mathbb{Q}$) and uncountable ($\mathbb{R}$) infinities is not known to ancient philosophers.

The first philosophers view infinity either as a characteristic or as a bearer of characterisations. The latter usage is prominent in Anaximander, who understands *apeiron* as the basic substance out of which everything comes into being and into which it dissolves again. By contrast, for Aristotle *apeiron* is an attribute of number and magnitude and hence incapable of independent existence.

Zeno attempts to show in several of his paradoxes that conceptualising multitudes as well as magnitudes of finite things entangles us in the assumption that they are also infinite and thus characterised simultaneously by opposing features. As we saw earlier, Zeno shows in DK29B3 that things that we take to be of finite number are also of an infinite number. And things we take to be of a finite size, such as a certain physical body, also have to be assumed to be of infinite size (DK29B1), for we can always go on to divide it into further parts and each of these parts will have some 'magnitude and thickness'. We saw earlier that in the runner paradox, Zeno shows that a finite extension to be covered also has to be conceived as being infinitely divisible,[208] and thus seems to leave the runner to cover infinitely many spatial parts. In all these cases, Zeno thinks we face the problem that something finite is also infinite, which is seen as paradoxical.

Aristotle reacts to Zeno's motion paradoxes by trying to show that the seemingly dubious alliance finite things have with infinity is unproblematic if conceived in the right way. He first distinguishes explicitly different kinds of infinity – most importantly infinity of division from infinity of addition.[209] According to Aristotle, Zeno did not sufficiently distinguish between the two so that from an always continuing division of a continuous stretch Zeno wrongly

---

[208] Scholarship in the first half of the twentieth century assumed that Zeno's paradoxes about infinite divisibility attempt to challenge also the mathematicians.

[209] He is also aware of convergent infinite series; see *Physics* 206b3–9.

infers an infinite extension.[210] Aristotle attempts to show that assuming an infinite extension, and especially an infinite body, is inconsistent (he argues for the universe to be finite).[211] Infinite divisibility, by contrast, which he explicitly claims to come from the mathematicians (203b15–30), is the main reason we cannot exclude the idea of infinity *tout court*. Continuous magnitudes are indeed always further divisible, Aristotle assumes. But this does not mean that they can have been divided wherever they are divisible (among other things, several of the possible parts derived from division will overlap, so we cannot derive all these overlapping parts at any given time). And more generally, for Aristotle the process of division can always go on but will never lead to an end. For him the infinity of division is only a potential infinity, not one that can be fully actualized.[212]

Fitting with his assessment of mathematics as a secure science, Aristotle is eager to show that his finitist conception of the universe can preserve the infinity the mathematicians in fact need for their practise (207b27ff.). According to Aristotle, the mathematicians do not really need an actual infinity; all they need is that any given line can be further extended or further divided, and there can always be a greater number than any assigned number (for any integer n there can be an integer $n + 1$)[213] – all of which for him belong to the potential infinite.

A final look at Euclid's usage of the infinite in the *Elements* shows that the fundamental philosophical discussions about infinity are interestingly absent from mathematical thinking of the time. On the one hand, infinite divisibility, which Aristotle claims to be important for the mathematicians and which Zeno's paradoxes put into question, is not explicitly formulated (though implicitly assumed in ancient mathematics, as shown by *On Indivisible Lines*).[214] The place where we may assume infinite divisibility to be explicitly in play (and to find some affinity to philosophical discussions) is the method of exhaustion. It is used in several propositions in *Elements*, Book XII, and shows that a figure can

---

[210] Zeno seems to assume that infinite division may lead to infinitely many non-converging extended parts which, added back together, would lead to an infinitely extended whole – Aristotle analyses this inference as a lack of distinguishing strictly between infinity of addition and division (233a21 ff.).

[211] For Aristotle, there cannot be an infinite body, since body is defined as what is *limited* by a surface; and there cannot be an infinite number since number is what can be counted.

[212] It is potential in a very specific way, see Sattler (2020b). For Aristotle, not *every* part that can potentially be conceived can thus be actually there, but *any* part can be actualized. Consequently, the whole continuum cannot be thought of as the sum of its parts, if by this we mean that all the parts are given prior to the sum.

[213] There 'can be', not there 'exists' an integer $n + 1$, otherwise, infinitely many integers would exist, which goes against Aristotle's finitist conception that does not allow for an actually existing infinite magnitude or multitude.

[214] Infinite divisibility is also discussed by later authors, like Geminus and Proclus, in the context of commenting on Euclid I, 10.

be approximated by a sequence of other, smaller figures inscribed inside it. For example, we 'square' a circle by continuously inscribing a sequence of regular polygons inside it, starting with a square, seemingly going on ad infinitum. However, Euclid stops after a small number of steps here, just enough to show that the difference between the original figure and the inscribed figure decreases by at least half at each step of the sequence. Accordingly, there is no talk about infinity here; Euclid does not tell us to continue always further.

On the other hand, Euclid assumes infinity in multitude and magnitude in the *Elements* in a way that does not suggest any conceptual difficulties with it; for example, for Euclid there exist infinitely many commensurable and incommensurable straight lines (*Elements* X, def. 3). And he even assumes infinity in cases where strictly speaking it is not needed, such as in I, 12, where it is 'required to draw a straight line perpendicular to the given infinite straight line *AB* from the given point *C*, which is not on *AB*' – here the given line is infinite, but in fact we can use a line of whatever size we choose; we do not need an infinite line.

There is one place in the *Elements*, however, where the employment of infinity is indeed necessary. In Book I, definition 23, parallels are defined with the help of infinity: 'Parallel lines are straight lines which, being in the same plane, and being produced to infinity in each direction, meet with one another in neither (of these directions).' And the fifth postulate in Book I claims that 'if a straight line falling on two straight lines makes the interior angles on the same side less than two right angles, the two straight lines, if produced to infinity, meet on that side on which are the angles less than the two right angles' (we are dealing with geometries only of flat spaces here); see also I, 29.

This is the only context where Aristotle's suggestion does not seem to work, that mathematicians do not really need lines of infinite length but only of arbitrarily long length. For if we assume that the lines are not extended to infinity but only as long as we please, too many pairs of lines will count as parallel and thus falsify postulate 5. Hussey has suggested a modal reworking for Aristotelian finitists.[215] But in Euclid, we do not find any such reworking, nor any sign of the fundamental philosophical debate about infinity. While philosophers of the classical time take mathematics as the main example to discuss what makes for a secure science, mathematicians at least in part ignore their philosophical considerations.

---

[215] Hussey (1993) suggests to rework definition 23 as follows: '*Parallel* straight lines are those, which being in the same plane, are such that it is not possible that there should be a length L such that, if the lines are produced in either direction to a length L, they meet'; so we would need to work with a modal operator such as 'it is not possible that'.

References

The Presocratic fragments, where possible, refer to the edition by Diels and Kranz. For Plato's works, the Stephanus page numbers are given, for Aristotle's, the Bekker pagination. Translations are from the following editions (sometimes with slight modifications).

Editions

Annas, Julia (1976), *Aristotle's* Metaphysics *Books M and N*, Clarendon Press.
Aristotle (1995), *The Complete Works of Aristotle*: *The Revised Oxford Translation*, edited by Jonathan Barnes, Princeton University Press.
Barnes, Jonathan (1993), *Aristotle's* Posterior Analytics (second edition), Clarendon Press.
Diels, Hermann, and Kranz, Walther (eds.) (1951), *Fragmente der Vorsokratiker*, Weidmannsche Verlagsbuchhandlung.
Heath, Thomas (1956), *Euclid, The Thirteen Books of the Elements*, translated with introduction and commentary, volumes I–III, Dover.
Huffman, Carl (1993), *Philolaus of Croton: Pythagorean and Presocratic*, Cambridge University Press.
 (2005), *Archytas of Tarentum*, Cambridge University Press.
Hussey, Edward (1993), *Aristotle's* Physics *Books III and IV*, Clarendon Press.
Kirk, Geoffrey S., Raven, John E., and Schofield, Malcolm (eds.) (1983), *The Presocratic Philosophers* (second edition), Cambridge University Press. [KRS]
Lee, Henry D. P. (ed.) (1967), *Zeno of Elea*, translation with notes, Hakkert.
Plato (1997), *Complete Works*, ed. John Cooper, Hackett.
Vitrac, Bernard (1990–2001), *Euclide d'Alexandrie*, Les Éléments, volumes I–IV, Presses Universitaires de France.

Secondary Literature

Acerbi, Fabio (2013), 'Aristotle and Euclid's Postulates', *Classical Quarterly* 63(2), 680–685. DOI: https://doi.org/10.1017/S0009838813000177.
 (2020), 'Mathematical Generality, Letter-Labels, and All That', *Phronesis* 65(1), 27–75. DOI: https://doi.org/10.1163/15685284-12342029.
Annas, Julia (1987), 'Die Gegenstände der Mathematik bei Aristoteles', in Andreas Graeser (ed.), *Mathematics and Metaphysics in Aristotle*, P. Haupt Publishers, pp. 131–147.

Balme, David M. (1987), 'The Place of Biology in Aristotle's Philosophy', in Allan Gotthelf & James G. Lennox (eds.), *Philosophical Issues in Aristotle's Biology*, Cambridge University Press, pp. 9–20.

Baron, Samuel (2021), 'Mathematical Explanation: A Pythagorean Proposal', *The British Journal for the Philosophy of Science*, 75(3), 1–29.

Broadie, Sarah (2021), *Plato's Sun-Like Good*, Cambridge University Press.

Burkert, Walter (1972), *Lore and Science in Ancient Pythagoreanism*, trans. Edwin L. Minar, Cambridge University Press.

Burnyeat, Myles (2000), 'Plato on Why Mathematics is Good for the Soul', in Timothy Smiley (ed.), *Mathematics and Necessity: Essays in the History of Philosophy*, The British Academy, pp. 1–81.

Chemla, Karine (2024), 'The Dark Side of the History of Proof', in Bharath Sriraman (ed.), *Handbook of the History and Philosophy of Mathematical Practice*, Springer, pp. 2137–2161. DOI: https://doi.org/10.1007/978-3-030-19071-2_81-1.

Cleary, John (1985), 'On the Terminology of "Abstraction" in Aristotle', *Phronesis*, 30(1), 13–45.

Cuomo, Serafina (2001), *Ancient Mathematics*, London: Routledge.

De Risi, Vincenzo (2021), 'Euclid's Common Notions and the Theory of Equivalence', *Foundations of Science* 26, 301–324.

Harari, Orna (2003), 'The Concept of Existence and the Role of Constructions in Euclid's *Elements*', *Archive for History of Exact Sciences* 57, pp. 1–23. DOI: https://doi.org/10.1007/s004070200053.

—— (2008), 'Proclus' Account of Explanatory Demonstrations in Mathematics and Its Context', *Archiv für Geschichte der Philosophie* 90, 137–164.

Heath, Thomas L. (1921), *A History of Greek Mathematics*, Oxford University Press.

Hellman, Geoffrey, and Stewart Shapiro (2018), *Varieties of Continua*, Oxford University Press.

Horsten, Leon (2022), 'Philosophy of Mathematics', *The Stanford Encyclopedia of Philosophy*, Edward N. Zalta (ed.), https://plato.stanford.edu/archives/spr2022/entries/philosophy-mathematics/.

Jope, James (1972), 'Subordinate Demonstrative Science in the Sixth Book of Aristotle's *Physics*', *Classical Quarterly* 22, 279–292.

Klein, Jacob (1968), *Greek Mathematical Thought and the Origin of Algebra*, trans. Eva Brann, Massachusetts Institute of Technology Press.

Knorr, Wilbur Richard (1975), *The Evolution of the Euclidean Elements*, Reidl.

Lang, Marc (2021), 'What Could Mathematics Be for It to Function in Distinctively Mathematical Scientific Explanations?', *Studies in History and Philosophy of Science* 87, 44–53.

References

Lear, Jonathan (1982), 'Aristotle's Philosophy of Mathematics', *Philosophical Review* 91, 161–192.

Lennox, James (2021), 'Aristotle's Biology', *The Stanford Encyclopedia of Philosophy* (Fall 2021 Edition), Edward N. Zalta (ed.), https://plato.stanford.edu/archives/fall2021/entries/aristotle-biology/.

Mancosu, Paolo, Francesca Poggiolesi, and Christopher Pincock (2023), 'Mathematical Explanation', *The Stanford Encyclopedia of Philosophy*, Edward N. Zalta & Uri Nodelman (eds.), https://plato.stanford.edu/archives/fall2023/entries/mathematics-explanation/.

Manders, Kenneth (2008), 'The Euclidean Diagram', in Paolo Mancosu (ed.), *Philosophy of Mathematical Practice*, Clarendon Press, pp. 112–183.

McKirahan, Richard D. (1992), *Principles and Proofs: Aristotle's Theory of Demonstrative Science*, Princeton University Press.

Mendell, Henry (2004), 'Aristotle and Mathematics', *Stanford Encyclopaedia of Philosophy*, Edward N. Zalta (ed.), https://plato.stanford.edu/archives/spr2017/entries/aristotle-mathematics/.

—— (2022), 'Plato on Mathematics', in David Ebrey and Richard Kraut (eds.), *The Cambridge Companion to Plato*, pp. 358–398, Cambridge University Press.

Menn, Stephen (2002), 'Plato and the Method of Analysis', *Phronesis* 47(3), 193–223. DOI: https://doi.org/10.1163/15685280260458127.

Mueller, Ian (1969), 'Euclid's *Elements* and the Axiomatic Method', *The British Journal for the Philosophy of Science* 20, 289–309.

—— (1974), 'Greek Mathematics and Greek Logic', in John Corcoran (ed.), *Ancient Logic and Its Modern Interpretations*, Synthese Historical Library, vol. 9, pp. 35–70, Springer.

—— (1980), 'Ascending to Problems: Astronomy and Harmonics in *Republic* VII', in John Peter Anton (ed.), *Science and the Sciences in Plato*, Delmar, pp. 103–122.

—— (1981), *Philosophy of Mathematics and Deductive Structure in Euclid's Elements*, MIT Press.

Netz, Reviel (1999), *The Shaping of Deduction in Greek Mathematics*, Cambridge University Press.

Neugebauer, Otto (1936), *Studien zur Geschichte der antiken Algebra III* (Quellen und Studien zur Geschichte der Mathematik, Abteilung B: Studien 3).

—— (1969), *Vorlesungen über Geschichte der antiken mathematischen Wissenschaften 1, Vorgriechische Mathematik* (second edition). Grundlehren der mathematischen Wissenschaften, vol. 43, Springer.

Proclus (1992), *A Commentary on the First Book of Euclid's Elements*, trans. Glenn R. Morrow, Princeton University Press.

References

Restrepo, Guillermo, and Villaveces, José (2012), 'Mathematical Thinking in Chemistry', *Hyle* 18(1), 3–22.

Salmon, Wesley (1980), *Space, Time and Motion: A Philosophical Introduction*, Dickenson Publishing Company.

Sattler, Barbara M. (2012), 'A Likely Account of Necessity, Plato's Receptacle as a Physical and Metaphysical Basis of Space', *Journal of the History of Philosophy* 50(2), 159–195.

(2019), 'The Notion of Continuity in Parmenides', *Philosophical Inquiry* 43 (1/2), 40–53.

(2020a), *The Concept of Motion in Ancient Greek Thought*, Cambridge University Press.

(2020b), 'Divisibility or Indivisibility: The Notion of Continuity from the Presocratics to Aristotle', in Stewart Shapiro and Geoffrey Hellman (eds.), *The History of Continuity: Philosophical and Mathematical Perspectives*, pp. 6–26, Oxford University Press.

(2021), 'Paradoxes as Philosophical Method and their Zenonian Origins', *Proceedings of the Aristotelian Society* 121(2), 153–181.

Scott, Dominic (2006), *Plato's* Meno, Cambridge University Press.

Simplicius (2002), *On Aristotle* Physics 3, trans. James O. Urmson, Bloomsbury.

Simplicius (2011), *On Aristotle* Physics 1.3–4, trans. C. C. W. Taylor and Pamela M. Huby, Bloomsbury.

Szabó, A. (2004), 'Wie ist die Mathematik zu einer deduktiven Wissenschaft geworden?', in Jean Christianidis (ed.), *Classics in the History of Greek Mathematics*, pp. 45–80. Springer (first published in 1956).

Tannery, Paul (1884), 'Sur l'authenticité des axiomes d'Euclide', *Bulletin des Sciences Mathématiques et Astronomiques*, Series 2, 8(1), 162–175.

(1887), *La geometrie grecque*, Gauthier-Villars.

Unguru, Sabetai (1975), 'On the Need to Rewrite the History of Greek Mathematics', *Archive for History of Exact Sciences* 15, 67–114.

von Fritz, Kurt (1955), 'Die *Archai* in der griechischen Mathematik', *Archiv für Begriffsgeschichte* 1, 12–103.

(1970), 'The Discovery of Incommensurability by Hippasus of Metapontum', in David Furley and Reginald E. Allen (eds.), *Studies in Presocratic Philosophy* 1, 211–231, Routledge.

Zeuthen, Hieronymus G. (1896), *Geschichte der Mathematik in Altertum und Mittelalter*, A. D. Höst.

Acknowledgements

I want to thank Stewart Shapiro for encouraging me to write this Element; two anonymous readers for the press for their helpful suggestions; Henry Mendell for conversations on the relationship of Greek mathematics to its Babylonian and Egyptian forerunners, Salomon Ofmann for conversations on incommensurability; Christian Tapp and Gottfried Heinemann for valuable feedback on individual sections, and especially Vera-Maria Erdmann and Steven Wagner for reading the whole manuscript. Vera-Maria Erdmann also helped to make some of my drawings and ideas computer-readable.

I dedicate this Element to the memory of my grandfather, A. Leichtfried, who taught me reading, writing, and arithmetic before I started school.

Cambridge Elements =

The Philosophy of Mathematics

Penelope Rush
University of Tasmania

From the time Penny Rush completed her thesis in the philosophy of mathematics (2005), she has worked continuously on themes around the realism/anti-realism divide and the nature of mathematics. Her edited collection, *The Metaphysics of Logic* (Cambridge University Press, 2014), and forthcoming essay 'Metaphysical Optimism' (*Philosophy Supplement*), highlight a particular interest in the idea of reality itself and curiosity and respect as important philosophical methodologies.

Stewart Shapiro
The Ohio State University

Stewart Shapiro is the O'Donnell Professor of Philosophy at The Ohio State University, a Distinguished Visiting Professor at the University of Connecticut, and Professorial Fellow at the University of Oslo. His major works include *Foundations without Foundationalism* (1991), *Philosophy of Mathematics: Structure and Ontology* (1997), *Vagueness in Context* (2006), and *Varieties of Logic* (2014). He has taught courses in logic, philosophy of mathematics, metaphysics, epistemology, philosophy of religion, Jewish philosophy, social and political philosophy, and medical ethics.

About the Series

This Cambridge Elements series provides an extensive overview of the philosophy of mathematics in its many and varied forms. Distinguished authors will provide an up-to-date summary of the results of current research in their fields and give their own take on what they believe are the most significant debates influencing research, drawing original conclusions.

Cambridge Elements ☰

The Philosophy of Mathematics

Elements in the Series

Mathematical Pluralism
Graham Priest

The Mereology of Classes
Gabriel Uzquiano

Iterative Conceptions of Set
Neil Barton

Introducing the Philosophy of Mathematical Practice
Jessica Carter

Elements of Purity
Andrew Arana

Husserl's Philosophy of Mathematical Practice
Mirja Hartimo

Definitions and Mathematical Knowledge
Andrea Sereni

Medieval Finitism
Mohammad Saleh Zarepour

Mathematics is (mostly) Analytic
Gregory Lavers

Mathematical Notations
Dirk Schlimm

Abstractionism
Francesca Boccuni and Luca Zanetti

Philosophy of Mathematics from the Pythagoreans to Euclid
Barbara M. Sattler

A full series listing is available at: www.cambridge.org/EPM

For EU product safety concerns, contact us at Calle de José Abascal, 56–1°,
28003 Madrid, Spain or eugpsr@cambridge.org.